Holding **Your Family** Together

I don't have a wife yet, and certainly no babies—but when I one day have a family, I'd love to try this! It seems like superglue, holding families together.

Janakan Arulkumarasan
Founder and CEO, Onoko International, Hong Kong

Rich Melheim is a dynamic and brilliant analyst and communicator who opens hearts and minds of children, families and everyone he meets to greater truth, wisdom and understanding. I recommend Rich and his writings for all who want to understand life better and grow in wisdom, knowledge and discernment.

Dr. Ted Baehr
Founder and CEO, www.movieguide.org
Hollywood, California

The FAITH5 methods and materials, when implemented to the way they are designed in the family, go a long way to solving the problem of biblical literacy. Rich honors me by being my friend.

Dr. Tony Campolo
Professor Emeritus, Eastern University
St. Davids, Pennsylvania

These are some of the most exciting and effective models I've seen to connect the Church, the home and the gospel. I strongly recommend the use of this every-night-in-every-home material.

Dr. Bill Easum
President, 21st Century Strategies, Inc., www.effectivechurch.com
Corpus Christi, Texas

A beautifully warm and engaging book full of hope, wisdom and experience. A must-read for anyone with a love or concern for young people and family.

Peter Eckermann
Vetamorphus Coordinator SA, Elev8 Youth Ltd.
O'Halloran Hill, South Australia

This book offers Christian parents an inspired plan to build spiritual truth and health into the lives of children. Dr. Rich offers practical ways to bless your children, draw them close to God, and counteract a culture that robs kids of the security you long to provide.

Lana Ensrud
Former Executive Director, Life Coaches for Kids®
Brooklyn Center, Minnesota

Dr. Rich Melheim's beautifully crafted book motivates, guides, teaches and challenges us to create and maintain positive, nurturing relationships with our children. By integrating FAITH5 into our day-to-day routines, our family relationships will grow with resilience and be a true blessing and valuable investment for our children's lives and future generations.

Karen Felker
Clinical Placement Coordinator in Higher Education
Wheaton College, Wheaton, Illinois

In *Holding Your Family Together,* Rich Melheim shares the distilled wisdom of a thousand conversations filtered through a life lived at the edge of eternity. Rich's brilliance is apparent in his art, his musical composition, his speaking, his writing and his careful listening. He offers a simple and practical pattern for creating relationships with your children that you will never regret. The genius of FAITH5 is flawless. Here is the secret for assuring that your faith will pass from generation to generation. Following these steps daily will implant values and affections that will endure forever.

Dr. Carl George
Founder, MetaChurch and Consulting for Growth, Inc.
Taylors, South Carolina

There is a desperate need today for tools to help families regroup at the end of the day so God's design for the family is not compromised. *Holding Your Family Together* is a simple tool that parents can use to celebrate the ups and the downs, stay connected and shape their children to walk in the way of the Lord. This book is a must-read for every family who wants to maintain the bond of love and leave a legacy that is never forgotten in the hearts of their children.

Dr. Paul R. Gupta
President, HBI Global Partners
Chennai, India

Reader alert! When you plunge into this book you'll laugh out loud, cry sentimentally and unabashedly, and marvel at the new insights you gain. Get ready to read this all in one sitting—it's that good! Rich Melheim has woven his personal bibliography, the stories of many others, deep biblical and theological insight, and the latest in brain science into a compelling case for living the spiritual practices he calls FAITH5. Doing these practices will be good for you, your family, your kids, your marriage and your physical and spiritual life.

Dr. Paul Hill
Executive Director, Vibrant Faith Ministries
Minneapolis, Minnesota

Rich's love and concern for wholesome families is evident in his writings. I highly recommend this book.

Reverend C. D. Jebasingh
Founder and President, Galilean International
Mumbai, India

What a beautiful and utterly compelling book! But it is much more than just another great read; it is a powerful tool for all who are looking for the right routines to create and maintain happy, godly families. Rich Melheim's creative abilities, as well as his fresh insight into science and his solid foundation in the Word of God, will change the way you raise your children one prayer at a time, one care at a time, and one night at a time.

Stephan Joubert
Extraordinary Professor in Contemporary Ecclesiology,
University of the Free State, South Africa
Research Fellow, Radboud University, Nijmegen, The Netherlands

The West meets the East in Rich. Rich also makes everyone he meets feel spiritually and emotionally rich (uplifted), just as his name. It was such an honor and pleasure to be his advisor and friend. I can't wait to introduce this Rich-ness and FAITH5 to Asia!

Dr. B. J. Jun
Director of International Affairs, Asian Center for Theological Studies and Missions (ACTS), Seoul, Korea

In *Holding Your Family Together*, Rich has brought together Word and service, congregation and family, content and experience, and peer and adult mentorship. This is a pedagogical strategy that is faithful to the gospel and highly effective in making disciples and preparing them for their vocations in the world.

Dr. Roland Martinson
Academic Dean, Luther Seminary
St. Paul, Minnesota

Back in home in Africa, I recall how the toll of the family bell woke us up at 6:00 AM and gathered us at 9:00 PM daily to talk, sing and pray together. As I look back, I acknowledge how this routine positively impacted my life. I am convinced that much of the dysfunction plaguing our world would be history if every home imbibed the spirit of FAITH5. This may very well be the way to heal our world and make it a better place for all of the human race. Thank you, Rich, for this invaluable family resource.

Olukayode Olubunmi
Founder and CEO, Okayhouse Film, Television and Records
Los Angeles, CA and Lagos, Nigeria

This book contains simple, easy-to-follow and quick routines that every parent must put into practice each day. These routines will have a lasting impact on their children and the future generation while instilling godly values in them.

David Peters
CEO, Cephas Media Group, Mumbai, India

I simply have never seen a book like this. I was blown away by it. Northwood Church will definitely promote this among our families. Everyone talks about "discipling" your family, but Rich takes it a step further and provides a tool with which we can do that. Every family seeking to follow Jesus should read this and implement it. I'm a soon-to-be-first-time grandfather—my kids will read this!

Bob Roberts, Jr.
Senior Pastor, Northwood Church, Keller, Texas
Author, *Bold as Love; Transformation: How Glocal Churches Transform Lives and the World;* and *Glocalization: How Followers of Jesus Engage a Flat World*

There are books that make good airplane books. There are books that are bedside books and coffee table books. Then there are those rare books that belong on the kitchen counter or in the family room, within easy reach for constant consultation and inspiration. Rich Melheim has written such a book.

Dr. Leonard Sweet
Bestselling Author and Professor, Drew University (George Fox University)
Chief Contributor, sermons.com
Orcas Island, Washington

HOLDING
YOUR
FAMILY
TOGETHER

5 Simple Steps to Help
Bring Your Family Closer to
God and Each Other

Dr. Rich Melheim

BETHANYHOUSE
a division of Baker Publishing Group
Minneapolis, Minnesota

© 2013 by Rich Melheim

Published by Bethany House Publishers
11400 Hampshire Avenue South
Bloomington, Minnesota 55438
www.bethanyhouse.com

Bethany House Publishers is a division of
Baker Publishing Group, Grand Rapids, Michigan

Bethany House edition published 2015
ISBN 978-0-7642-1522-3

Previously published by Regal Books.

Printed in the United States of America

Library of Congress Control Number: 2014956641

15   16   17   18   19   20   21   7   6   5   4   3   2   1

To the memory of Pastor Ray and Kathryn Melheim,
two wonderful parents who taught me how to live in Christ,
taught me how to die in Christ, and still shepherd and
enrich my life a little every day.

 Share ....

 Read ....

 Talk ....

 Pray ....

 Bless ....

Contents

The Dream and the Plan

*He will turn the hearts of parents to their children and the
hearts of children to their parents.*
MALACHI 4:6

Imagine raising a daughter who wouldn't think of going to bed
without talking to you about her highs and lows every night, even
though she's 16.

Imagine raising a son who won't turn out the lights without
asking you about *your* day, praying for *your* highs and lows, and
blessing *you*.

Imagine growing up in a home where everyone feels loved, valued and heard every night; a family that seeks God's wisdom, will
and Word at the center of their lives; an intimate community where
every night is an experience of caring, sharing, comfort and peace.

Does this sound like an impossible dream?

It isn't.

Does it sound like an improbable dream?

Maybe.

One thing is for sure: This dream is not going to magically mate-
rialize without intention, commitment and a workable plan on your
part to make it happen. Having a close and caring family is a beautiful dream, but a dream without a plan isn't worth a nickel. However,
a dream *with* a workable plan may be worth a million bucks.

Listen to the Scripture song "Sun of Righteousness" at www.faith5.org/extras.

Your Plan: The FAITH5™

In the pages of this book, I am going to give you such a plan to hold your family together and a way to create a healthy, happy, secure and godly family one night at a time. With this plan, I believe you will make significant strides in turning your home into a place your children will one day describe as an island of fun, security, support, love, wisdom and deep peace. To do this, I will take you through five steps to implement with your children during the next six weeks:

Step 1:   SHARE your highs and lows every night.

Step 2:   READ a key Bible verse or story every night.

Step 3:   TALK about how the Bible reading might relate to your highs and lows every night.

Step 4:   PRAY for one another's highs and lows aloud every night.

Step 5:   BLESS one another before turning out the lights on the day.

Simple, huh? Actually, it is. The hardest part is not coming up with the plan but starting it and following through with it for the first few nights. After that, it gets easier and a lot more fun. My staff and I call this plan FAITH5, or "Faith Acts in the Home." When you use this simple nightly routine intentionally and consistently over time, it will help you model compassion, empathy, reflection and care for your children.

Your Personal Research Assistant

To show you how FAITH5 works, on the first page of each chapter I begin with a story of real people who tested the process for six weeks.

Many of these families did so under difficult situations, and they will show you how they were able to follow the steps. Of course, the real question is not whether FAITH5 works for *others*, but whether it will work for *you*. Will it help hold your family together?

What if you're a single mom? What if you're a dad working a second shift and can't physically be with your kids at bedtime? What if you are half a world away in the military or on a long-term assignment? What if you're separated from your own children physically or emotionally and have limited access? What if you're a grandparent and the only healthy spiritual influence in their lives? What if your kids are raised and don't include God in their lives at all? What if you have a teenager who doesn't talk to you and you fear it is already too late?

First, let me encourage you that *anything* you do is better than nothing. Any conversation, any sharing, any prayer is better than none. Even if you simply start with a conversation such as, "Tell me your high and low of the day," opening this door will be the first step to relational health. This little crack in the conversational dike can lead to a flood of deeper and more meaningful sharing. The art of the start is a true art indeed, and you never know where it can lead. So get into the game. Get out on the field. The ball isn't going to come to you if you are sitting in the stands. (Okay, it might come to you, but it won't count!)

Second, to assist in answering these questions and to equip you for success, I'm going to expose you to a world of wonderful resources. I'll pepper a little psychology, a little sociology, a little neurology and a little theology into this book. I will also be adding a few choice links to some of the best online articles and resources I came across during my three-year doctoral dissertation process. Consider these links as portals to a whole lot of people who are a lot smarter than me. Use them, and you will be guilty of what I call "brilliance by association!"

Third, let me suggest that you don't read this book alone. Just as parenting is easier when you can surround your child with a community of aunts, uncles, grandparent figures and cousins, creating a healthy system to surround and support you in your journey to healthy parenting will make the process a joy and a blessing. Remember that "dead" is another word for "martyr." Don't like that word? Then don't take on the daunting task of parenting alone!

All you really need for an asylum is a big room and the right kind of people.

MESSAGE ON A BUMPER STICKER

Your Dream Team

By far, the best way to get exceptional results from this book is to read it with a Dream Team of people you know, love and trust. These should be people who will commit to building their families as you work toward building yours. They should be individuals who will share their highs, lows, victories and struggles with you on a regular basis. They should be people who will keep you accountable, like they do in Weight Watchers and AA. Discussing the themes each week among trusted friends and adding that extra ounce of encouragement, fellowship and accountability into the six-week process can make all the difference between walking away from the book with a couple of good ideas and walking away with a healthier family and a new team of supporters.

Please consider me the first member of your Dream Team and your own personal research assistant. To enhance your Dream Team time even further, we have created a FAITH5 Blog (faith5.org/blog), a six-week FAITH5 Course (faith5.org/course) and a FAITH5 Facebook site to share stories, struggles and strivings with real people who tell their stories of how FAITH5 is enriching their family lives. Go to Facebook and search for FAITH5, and then "friend" me so we can talk if you have questions.

Your Investment

I am not going to ask you to *spend* any time with your children, because when you spend something it is gone. Instead, I'm going to challenge you to *invest* your time in your children. What is the investment? Don't pull out your wallet—your money isn't good enough. All the money in the world can't buy this dream. Rather, pull out your watch and your calendar. During the next six weeks, I am going to ask you to invest your most precious non-renewable currency (your time) and aim it at your most priceless God-given blessing (your family) and your most essential and important responsibility— holding your family together in a world that could tear it apart.

Try this plan for 42 nights, using one chapter of the book each week as your discussion guide and blueprint. See if it doesn't make a significant positive difference in your family communication and care. If you can't commit 42 nights, just try it for six weeks. If you aren't able to commit six weeks, just try it for a month and a half. ☺

Conception is a lot more fun than delivery.
FORMER FRENCH PREMIER GEORGES POMPIDOU

Conception and Delivery

Does this all sound like work to you? It is, but I believe that once you get started, you will find your nightly time together a whole lot of *fun*—especially if you do the program in the ways I suggest. Engaging the brain, body and the environment while tossing in a little pillow fight now and then is a great way to start.

It is my prayer that this little book will give you the tools, team and techniques to hold your family together. It is my belief that it will give you these gifts *if* you simply give the plan and your family the gifts of a little time and attention each night for the next six weeks.

So get moving! Turn off the television, log off the Internet, set the cell phones on silent, disconnect the weapons of mass distraction, and get ready to invest in your family. The One who began this good work in you will be faithful to complete it, but you still have to show up.

— Dr. Rich

Sleeping in Heavenly Peace

I will both lie down and sleep in peace; for you alone,
O Lord, make me lie down in safety.
PSALM 4:8

This book is all about hijacking your nightly routine, injecting the DNA of Jesus into the nucleus of your family cell, planting seeds of faith just before your kids drift off to sleep, and harnessing the untapped power of a good night's sleep to incubate faith in your children's hearts, minds and spirits one night at a time.

A FAITH5 Family Story

Ann and Alan Eustis were concerned when their first-grade daughter, Callie, could not sleep through the night and consistently crawled into bed with them.[1] One of Callie's classmates had been murdered by the mother's estranged boyfriend, and at night Callie both feared for her safety and that of her parents. A year later, Callie was still crawling in bed with her parents when they started doing FAITH5. Within weeks of beginning the practice, Callie was back in her own bed, sleeping soundly through the night.

To learn Psalm 4:8 in song and American Sign Language, go to www.faith5.org/intro/song.

"We thank God every day for FAITH5," says Ann, a professor of education at Towson State, with a twinkle and a tear in her eye. "I really believe this was grace. Perfect timing. This was the model. Callie doesn't go to sleep lacking now. She goes to sleep full, and that's a real answer to prayer. Yes, there was developmental growth, but there really was a spiritual healing."

Part I: Where It Began

My Homeschool Home

Allow me to explain the origin of my passion and plan to help you hold your family together. Ever since I was a little boy, I wanted to be a dad. I was born into the family of a wonderful teacher and a fantastic storyteller—two great role models who happened to be my parents. Because of their intentional and consistent care during our bedtime ritual, I fell asleep nearly every night of my young life with something special. I was blessed to close my little eyes in the sure and certain knowledge that my parents loved me, and in the safe and secure awareness of God's watchful tender power and awesome almighty arms. I believe your children can have these gifts as well.

My Mother the Teacher

I was blessed with a mother who read to her children every night. My mother, Kathryn Marie, was a teacher before she married a preacher, and her specialty was teaching inner-city kids how to read. She delighted in her work, saw it as a true calling and, though she decided to stay home to raise her children when they were young, went straight back to teaching once the last of her kids was out of the house. She literally remained a teacher to her dying day.

Every night in the Melheim home would end in the same way—with this classy teacher's private class in session. Mom would perch herself at the top of the stairs in our tidy two-story house—my sisters' room on one side of the stairs, and mine on the other. Every night the class would begin with her reading and reading. When we were young, she treated our sleepy little brains to books filled with poems and rhymes and cadence: *The Cat in the Hat; One Fish, Two Fish; Put Me in the Zoo* and *Green Eggs and Ham*. As we grew, she advanced to chapter books: *Pippi Longstocking, Mio, My Son, Sugar Creek Gang, The Bobbsey Twins* and *Hardy Boys Mysteries*.

Wonderful stuff!

I can still hear the echo of our frantic objections as she would finish a chapter and slam a book shut. "No! Please, please, please!" we would complain. "One more chapter! One more chapter! Please!"

Mom would smile her sly, satisfied smile and announce, "Okay, but you better get your jammies on early tomorrow night and brush your teeth or . . ."

"Yes! Yes! Yes! Anything! Anything! Please! Read more! One more chapter!"

Mom the teacher was truly wise. She made sure our two-story home was actually a thousand-story home. Long before we could read, we were hooked on being "booked" as she caught us, brought us and taught us to fall in love with stories, vocabulary and words and use our imaginations.

Mom incubated dreams and seeded behaviors in us by expanding our minds. In this way, she grew our futures one book at a time, one story at a time, and one night at a time. We weren't wealthy, but thanks to Mom we were very rich.

The Nightly Rituals

After reading, we would always say our prayers. From the top of the tiny house stairs to the bottom of our mom's hopeful heart, she led us through our nightly, "Now I lay me down to sleep" prayers. She followed this with a little song:

Dear Father in heaven, look down from above
Bless Mommy and Daddy and all those we love
Bless Gramma and Grampa and Richard and Ruth and Karen . . .

A list of loved ones, neighbors, cousins and friends followed. The DiBrito family across the alley always made it into our nightly intercessions: "God bless Roger, Billy, Monica, Debbie, Betty, Teresa, Denise, Bernadette, Dominic . . ."

Grandpa Ome usually made my "God Bless" list. This disheveled old widowed usher at church always snuck me Juicy Fruit. I would thank him, and he'd wink. I made sure I stuck it under the pew for safekeeping before my parents could notice and confiscate my clandestine candied contraband.

My turtle, Myrtle, made it into most prayers, as did the guppies in the fish tank atop the refrigerator, my missing hamster, and our slightly neurotic Siamese cat, Samantha. (I prayed for her in spite of my suspicions that she had something to do with my hamster's sudden and mysterious disappearance.)

Night by night our prayer list grew as we grew in awareness of our neighbors in need, missionaries in the field, and children with bloated bellies in hungry countries half a world away. Night by night our care list grew. Night by night our share list grew. Night by night our capacity to love grew, our faith grew, and we grew. The list grew on and on and on.

One prayer at a time.

One care at a time.

One night at a time.

The Blessing Touch

After prayers, Mom always gave us a kiss, a hug, a fluffed pillow, a quilt or blanket snugged and tugged, and a loving blessing: "God bless you. I love you. Good night." We closed our trusting eyes every night in the clear and present affirmation of who we were, whose we were, and just how much we were loved by Mom, Dad, our family, our neighbors, our church, the guppies and the great big God of the Universe.

Thanks to Mom, I decided that if I were ever blessed with children of my own, my family would also be blessed with such "mothering" care and the same *rich* and *enriching* rituals—which I like to call "enrichuals"—every night. We would read, read, read and read some more. We would pray, pray and pray. And we would bless, bless, bless and bless. Every night.

Dad, Dad, the Best I Ever Had

Along with a sneaky teacher mom, I was blessed with a storytelling dad. My dad, Raymond Edward, knew how to weave wonderful tales. Funderful tales. Thunderful tales.

The scrawny kid with a mischievous million-dollar smile and wavy brown hair was raised in Sioux City, Iowa, during the Great Depression. Dad grew up with a gang of neighborhood friends in a day when "gang" was a good term. The family, including five brothers and sisters, may have been broke, but it was never poor. Dad's family had each other. They had love. They also had a neighborhood full of crazy friends and supportive church family. Because of Dad's rich repertoire of bedtime stories, I grew up believing that a kid could have a whole lot of homemade fun with nary a nickel to his name.

After a brief stint on the railroad and three and a half years in the South Pacific, Dad gave his future to Jesus and found himself at college, at seminary and then in the middle of a Minnesota sugar beet field, planting a church from scratch. To grow that flock, Pastor Ray made regular home visits, knocking on doors after supper—sometimes three or four nights a week. Dad would often return home late, but he always made a point of trudging up the creaky wooden stairs to kiss and bless his children, even if we were asleep. If my memory serves correctly, he'd usually stop first in my sisters' room. By the time he got to me, he was often more than tired, but I'd still beg him to tell me a story.

Dad's stories were interesting, but they were even more so if he was tired while he was telling them. He would begin, and then he would yawn. I would elbow him awake and beg, "Dad! What happened next? What happened next?" The railroad engineer/soldier/preacher's most vivid stories were centered on his childhood gang of misfit entrepreneurs and on his life as a young decorated sergeant in the Philippine Islands during the darkest days of World War II.

The Sergeant and the Sumo Samurai

Here is one story I'll never forget. Dad began by saying, "I was out in the jungle alone. The marines had bombed, bombed, bombed this particular island before we ran ashore, but there were still some enemy soldiers hidden in the maze of coral caves. They were out there. We knew it.

"On one particular island on one particular night, there were rumors that a huge sumo-wrestler-sized Japanese soldier had been spotted in the jungle. This phantom was reported to have arms as big as garbage can lids and a Samurai sword at his side.

"On this dark evening I was on guard duty, alone at the edge of camp. Just me, the mosquitos and my M1 rifle. It was one of those hot, sweaty nights where your clothes stick to your body and the bugs buzz you insane. I was alone, dozing off..."

As Dad told the story, he yawned and nodded. I had to elbow him. "What happened next?" I said. "What happened next?"

Dad resumed. "[Yawn] Well, I was peering out into the jungle when the moon slid behind the clouds and all was suddenly pitch black. Then, in the distance, I heard something that sounded like a sword or a machete hacking through the thick jungle grass. Whoosh, whoosh, whoosh, whoosh!

"I stared out, hoping and praying the moon would reappear! Whoosh, whoosh, whoosh! The sound was coming closer! Whoosh, whoosh! Closer! Closer! Closer!

"I squinted into the night as the moon slid from behind the clouds. A lump stuck in my throat. There in the tall grass not 50 feet away was this huge guy with a giant sword coming right toward me.

"I waited until he got within range. I lifted up my M1 and—click—the gun jammed! I ducked down into a foxhole as the sound came closer! Whoosh, whoosh! Closer! Whoosh, whoosh! Closer!"

Dad nodded off. I elbowed him again. "What happened next, Dad? What happened next?"

Dad yawned. "What happened next? I waited for what seemed like an eternity. I didn't dare move. I didn't dare breathe. I didn't dare flinch. Time stood suddenly still. I couldn't think. Had he left? Was he still there? Was I dreaming the whole thing?

"I finally got up enough nerve to peek over the foxhole. I found myself looking directly into his shins!"

Dad yawned.

"What happened next, Dad?" I shouted. "What happened next?"

"He..."

"WHAT?"

"He . . . cut . . . my head off."

"What?!"

Dad told the best stories. I decided that if I were ever blessed to be a father, I would do the same. We would read. We would pray. We would bless. And we would tell stories. Every night.

Jump Ahead Twenty Years

I was a new youth and family pastor. My Bible Camp sweetheart, Arlyce Joy, and I had been married for five years. She grew up in a little house on the Dakota prairie with seven brothers and sisters and wanted a big family. I had two sisters and, in spite of that fact, I also wanted to have children.

Arlyce and I paid off some bills. We did some traveling. For those first five years, unbeknownst to me, my wife squirreled away $50 a month from her paycheck and surprised me with a vacation to Hawaii for our fifth anniversary. Upon our return from the islands we decided, "Let's make a baby!"

Problems in Paradise

We spent the next year giddy, excited and happy, trying to make a baby at every chance we got. But it didn't happen the first year. Twelve months passed, but no baby. It didn't happen the second year, either. Twenty-four months passed, and no baby. It didn't happen in the third, fourth or fifth year. Thirty-six, 48 and then 60 months passed! Oh, baby, no baby!

Listen to Dr. Rich tell the story of "The Sergeant and the Sumo Samurai"
at www.faith5.org/intro/rich.

For 60 months we tried. For 60 months we prayed. For 60 months in a row the answer came back: "No, not you. Everyone else can have a child, but not you."

A Little Death

Infertility is no small matter. It is like experiencing a little death every month. Making love should be such a beautiful bonding thing, but ours became angry, tense and sad. As the biological clock ticked and ticked away month after frustrating month, it seemed less and less likely our prayers would be answered.

"Okay, it's that time of the month. Just do it!"

"Oh, that puts me in the mood."

Let me tell you: it almost destroyed our marriage.

Heightened Baby Awareness

During that time, everywhere I went I saw babies. I developed a heightened baby awareness. Almost like a homing device. I'd go to the park or the mall and there'd be babies. I'd go to the store and there'd be babies. Someone would be yelling at a child in the supermarket aisle and I would want to yank the kid away from him or her and yell, "Give me that child! You don't deserve to be a parent!"

During this time, two of my wife's sisters said, "Let's make a baby!" and bang! They were pregnant. My sister Karen and her husband Steve said, "Let's have a baby!" and bang! They were pregnant. Even my church president's 16-year-old daughter was—you guessed it—pregnant!

"Pastor Rich," she said, "we only did it once."

"Oh, shut up!"

Babies.

The Prayer Chain

A few years into this, the secretary of our church got wind we were having problems conceiving. Traveling back and forth to the Mayo Fertility Clinic every month was hard to keep under wraps.

We did everything we could to make a baby. Laparoscopies and hysterosalpingograms. Major abdominal surgery to suture up my wife's tipped uterus. Endometrial laser treatments to zap away her endometriosis. Nine months on one drug. Six months on another. Blind drug study.

It got to the point our church secretary, bless her heart, would come into my office with her calendar once a month, sporting a sheepish grin. "Oh, Pastor Rich," she would say, "it's that time of the month. You'd better go home early tonight. Would you like us to notify the prayer chain?"

Babies!

The Sixty-first Month

Oh, how I wanted to be a dad! We applied for adoption at two agencies and were moving up the lists when, on the sixty-first month, a little home pregnancy test turned green and blue in front of our eyes. We laughed and cried and fell on the bathroom floor, kissing and hugging in disbelief. I had to run right out and buy another. It, too, was positive. The awareness suddenly sunk in: we were going to have a baby! Then we got scared. What happens when you finally get what you want?

Trimester Tension

We knew the first months would be dangerous. A lot of babies are lost in the initial trimester. So we prayed, "God! Please get us through the first three months. We will thank You and praise You in every moment of parenting if You just get us through these first three."

Picture five-foot-nothing Arlyce Joy in the bathroom in a pink and blue terrycloth robe, leaning over the toilet at three in the morning, throwing up. "Braaaaaaagh! Thank ya, Jesus! Braaaagh! Thank ya, Jesus!"

We made it through the first trimester and were moving into the second. Our prayers shifted to, "Oh, please, God! Just get the baby up to two pounds. Two pounds . . . can You give me three?"

We made it through the second trimester and were moving into the third with all systems go. Momma was getting larger and larger and larger. Her feet were swelling. "Thank ya, Jesus!"

At the stroke of midnight on November 22, 1988, we wheeled into the hospital fully dilated—I think my wife mentioned Jesus that night, too. Twenty-six minutes later, just moments after the doctor arrived, "Waaaaaaaah!" out comes this beautiful bloody wrinkled lizard thing . . . and she was beautiful! She was the most beautiful bloody wrinkled lizard I ever saw. We named her Kathryn Elizabeth. I finally got to be a dad. Thank ya, Jesus.

Three years and another major surgery later, out came Joseph Martin. I was doubly blessed. Yes. Thank ya, thank ya, Jesus.

Mommying with a Mission and Daddying by Design

In gratitude for these priceless blessings, my wife and I decided we were going to be the best parents we could possibly be. So we began the gradual process of designing, crafting and creating marvelous and meaningful memories for our children—memories we wanted them to share every night of their lives. We wanted them to have memories that would mold them, shape them and hold them, even when they couldn't hold themselves. We wanted them to walk away with memories on the day they walked away from our graves.

We decided to plant the seeds for these positive memories in the fertile soil of a consistent nightly bedtime routine. Every night we were going to do a number of things intentionally right. We were going to give them the gifts of time and our full and complete attention. We were going to bless them with stories, songs, prayers, love, laughter, comfort, fun and security. To accomplish all this, we decided to do the following.

Share

We wanted to raise children who knew that their parents were always interested in their lives, so we committed to reflecting on the events of each day aloud together. Rather than simply asking, "How was your day?" and receiving a standard, "Fine," we would ask every member of the household—and even guests who happened to be there—to share both a high and a low every night.

Read

We wanted to raise children with marvelous, masterful vocabularies, an excellent command of language, and vivid imaginations. As a preschool director, Arlyce knew the invaluable gifts reading gives a child. As an amateur neurology hobbyist, I, too, knew what rhymes, cadence and stories could do to enrich busy little baby brains. There was no question reading and stories would be part of our nightly ritual.

Talk

We wanted to raise children who knew they could come to us with anything and who were in the practice of doing so regularly. To accomplish this, we decided to invest a few minutes each night discussing the highs and lows of their day and how to deal with and grow through them.

Pray

We wanted our little ones to grow into big ones who knew where to go with the concerns of the day. We wanted our children to have a clear and certain awareness of their heavenly Father, who would always be there for them, especially when their own parents were no longer around. To point them in this right direction, we were certainly going to pray.

Bless

I received a blessing every night growing up, and my little ones were going to get one too. I would kiss my pinky finger and trace a cross on their foreheads with special words every night. Sometimes the words were as simple as, "God bless you. I love you. Goodnight." Sometimes they were as eloquent as Aaron's blessing: "The Lord bless you and keep you" (Num. 6:24-26).

Sometimes I leaned a little liturgical: "Kathryn/Joseph, you have been sealed by the Holy Spirit and marked with the cross of Christ forever." Sometimes I shared a favorite phrase from a book title: "May you grow to be strong, loving and wise." Sometimes I blessed them with a promise written especially for them: "There is nothing you can ever say, and nothing you will ever do, that will ever stop God's awesome heart from always loving you. (And me and Mom, too!)"

Nearly every night ended with me heading into the hallway with a fun little chant:

> *I'm so happy to be your pappy.*
> *It don't bother to be your father.*
> *Flips my lid that you're my kid.*
> *I'm elated that we're related.*
> *Drives me WILD that you're my child.*
> *And Daddy will always love you, no matter what.*
> *Mommy will always love you, no matter what.*
> *Jesus will always love you, no matter what.*
> *God bless you, good night!*

The "no matter what" was especially important. I needed my kids to know the unconditional nature of Jesus' love. I also needed to remind myself of my vow to them and my promise to God to stay faithful to my calling as their father. I wanted them to walk away from my grave absolutely sure of my joy and honor to be their dad. I wanted them to give that same gift to their children, their children's children, and the great grandchildren I would never meet. I remember half-shouting, half-sobbing this same chant from the hallway on the last night before each child left for college. Ah, dads!

Part II: Exercise for Your Mind

Pillow Fight Every Night

In order to "fix" all these positive memories in my children's developing brains as they grew, I chose to add one additional item to our nightly "enrichuals." Contrary to all the standard bedtime wind-down parenting advice you may ever read or hear, I decided that my kids were going to have a pillow fight every night. I even made up a little song:

No children allowed to have fun tonight!
No children allowed for a pillow fight!

They would sing back:

Yes, children allowed to have fun tonight!
Yes, children allowed for a pillow fight!

As bedtime approached, we would sing this little ditty back and forth, and then I would announce, "All right! We'll have a pillow fight. But you'd better hustle upstairs and get your jammies on and teeth brushed, 'cause Daddy's a comin' up and he's going to be swinging!"

Up the stairs they'd dash in a flash, brush their teeth, throw on their pajamas, and then peek around the edge of the stairs. "We're reaaaaaaddy!" they'd shout.

I'd shout back, "Here comes Daddy! Ah, ha, ha!" Then, smash, crash, bang, boom! We'd be knocking over lamps. Knocking over kids. Knocking pictures off the wall. By grade school, I added bedside kickboxing to the nightly ritual. (Hey, couldn't hurt, right?)

Arlyce would be downstairs thinking, *Yeah, that's going to really get them ready for bed, isn't it? That's going to wind them down.*

But I knew a little something about psychology. And I knew a little something about sociology. And I knew a little something about neurology. Aside from the value of kids and parents being able to work out their displaced aggression on each other every night with a soft object, there were clear neurological benefits to adding a little exercise to the nightly routine prior to winding down.

Winding Up for a No-Whining Wind-down

Does winding up before winding down make any sense? Actually, it does. As it turns out, one of the best times to work out problems and fix positive memories in the human brain is *right after a workout.*

To listen to Dr. Rich's "Happy to Be Your Pappy Litany," go to www.faith5.org/extras.

Exercise enhances learning and brain functions by birthing new nerve cells and creating better connections between existing nerve cells. It lowers stress, reduces anxiety and depression, enhances the ability to focus, reduces ADD/ADHD, balances hormonal systems, bolsters immune systems, burns fat and slows aging processes way down.

Hmmm . . . sounds like parents might benefit from this, too?

A good workout prior to bedtime is actually a great wind-down from the day. It is also a good wind-up for what intentional and thoughtful parents should want to design into every night, which is:

- A recap of the day
- A recasting of the day's events in the context of a loving and supportive family
- A way to embed positive memories
- A sneaky method of short-circuiting any whining that might occur at bedtime
- A method of setting up the brain for maximum problem-solving abilities before drifting off to a better night's sleep

All this from some wiggles and giggles and hearts that race, from cares and prayers and a pillow in the face? You got it. An energetic wind-up is the perfect precursor to an effective wind-down. Don't believe it? Allow me to get technical and equip you with your first parental neurology lesson.

Oxygen, Glue and Attention, Too

There is a barrier between the brain and the blood called the "Blood Brain Barrier." (Creative title, huh?) This barrier only lets the smallest molecules through, blocking dangerous things like bacteria from entering the brain.

There are two molecules that pass through this barrier without any trouble at all: oxygen and glucose. Oxygen makes your brain alert and attentive. Glucose makes it retentive; it helps you remember. Oxygen removes something called "free radicals" from brain cells. These little guys eat up healthy cells and age the brain prematurely.

Glucose is like the glue that holds together your thoughts. It feeds the gray matter (glial cells) that nourish nerve cells, take waste products away, and send out little tracers telling nerves where to go, connect and grow.

You get the two marvelous molecules you need most to create and hold meaningful memories—oxygen and glucose—when you exercise.

Sopping Up the Toxic Spill

There is an area of the brain called the hippocampus that gives birth to baby nerve cells—neurons—by the thousands each night. (Most of these are born between the sixth and eighth hour of sleep.) This seahorse-shaped factory takes stem cells and turns them into these new nerves.

The hippocampus requires cortisol, a stress hormone, in small amounts to keep the body's fight-or-flight mechanisms ready. But when over-stressed, the body will overproduce cortisol. In large quantities, this chemical is toxic to baby neurons. Washed in stress hormones, they will wither and die.

Kisses, hugs, back rubs, stories, prayers, blessings and the assurance of love remove cortisol from the bloodstream. Exercise removes even more. If the body has exercised, the brain will give birth to two to three times more neurons. Following exercise, with cortisol levels diminished and even more oxygen and glucose in the brain, these newly birthed neurons have the best chance to grow and flourish.

Best Darn Nerve Fertilizer (BDNF)

Aside from sopping up cortisol and feeding brains oxygen and glucose, exercise releases the most powerful and beneficial brain-building, memory-fixing neurotransmitter of all: BDNF. There is a long and technical term for this magic nerve-enhancing molecule, but I like to simply call it the "Best Darn Nerve Fertilizer" you can ever spread across a brain and body to birth and hold positive memories.

As you exercise, the body releases massive doses of BDNF. This creates new neurons, grows new connections (synapses) at the ends of existing neurons, and fosters an explosion of new receptors at the ends of those nerves. According to Harvard psychiatrist Dr. John Ratey, BDNF molecules give nerve cells the tools they need to take in new information, process that information, associate it with existing knowledge, remember it, and put it into a context.

Setting the Stage for Solutions

Although the brain only makes up about 2 percent of your body weight and 16 percent of your body mass, it consumes 20 percent of your energy when at rest. After exercise, with all that BDNF coursing through the bloodstream with nothing to do, BDNF tends to congregate wherever the action is. If that action happens to be in the brain—a brain sharing highs and looking for solutions to the lows of the day—that's where the fertilizer will head.

The result is more nerve cells, more connections on the ends of the nerve cells, and more receptors on the ends of the connections of those nerve cells, all standing ready and available to help you sort out your problems. It's as if exercise builds a huge new super-highway for the transfer of information and puts a ton of cars on it, allowing you to share more information, look for solutions and build memories.

If you reflect on the day immediately *after* exercise and right *before* going to sleep, you set the stage for better sleep. Better yet, if you brainstorm innovative and creative solutions out loud with people who share their love and care, and then drift off to sleep in peace, you seed your dreams. This is the place where the brain does its best creative problem-solving work and where the Holy Spirit can whisper most powerfully to your child's heart, mind and spirit.

The Workout After the Workout

Here is one thing you need to know: Exercise adds adrenaline to the system, so it is essential to install a wind-down after the wind-up in order to get your children ready for sleep. After our pillow fight and kick-boxing matches each night—with all that oxygen, glucose and BDNF flooding through Kathryn's and Joseph's little brains—we would launch into an intentional wind-down routine. We would take turns sharing highs and lows, read, tell stories and talk. Then we would transition further into the more quiet and peaceful prayers and blessings.

Our babies ended each night with a kiss, a hug, a cross marked on their foreheads, songs of faith, and a blessing. They would close their eyes and drift off to sleep with all the toxic cortisol sopped out of their bloodstreams and all the healthy chemicals that love, security and safe touch provided into their dreams. Until, of course, they needed a glass or three of water, which, it turns out, moistens dehydrated lungs, allows capillaries to absorb more oxygen, washes away even more stress hormones, and is the cheapest and most effective lubricant you can buy (or get virtually free) to grow healthy brains.

Will FAITH5 Work for Your Family?

Over the years, FAITH5 and the fun we had with pillow fights were true gifts to the Melheim family. They helped to hold us on days we couldn't hold ourselves. It worked for us, but will FAITH5 work for your family? I believe it can and will.

During the last 20 years, my staff and I at Faith Inkubators have taught these concepts to tens of thousands of parents, kids, teachers and pastors in hundreds of cities in the United States, Australia, Korea and India. In the last decade, these nightly enrichuals have crystallized into a simple five-step process that any parent, grandparent, babysitter or guardian can easily tie into their existing nightly routine.

A few years ago, our brilliant family ministry consultant Debbie Streicher labeled these steps the FAITH5 (Faith Acts in the Home). They worked for my family. They are working for thousands of families across multiple continents tonight. I know they will work for you.

Five simple steps.

Five to 15 minutes a night—after the pillow fight!

One major change for good.

In the chapters that follow, we will look at the psychological, sociological, neurological and theological gifts these five simple steps can bring to enrich your evening rituals and help you hold your family together in powerful ways. Then, in the Epilogue, I will give you actual techniques for seeding dreams and accomplishing Christian education in your children's sleep. Stay tuned!

Dream Team Reflections

I will both lie down and sleep in peace; for you alone,
O Lord, make me lie down in safety.
PSALM 4:8

Gather with your family, friends or a small group of people you trust and respect to share the following:

Theme Verse
Read and highlight today's theme verse in your Bible, and then hop online to the link below to learn this verse in song and American Sign Language.

Reflection 1
What are your first memories of childhood? What do you remember about your room? Your bedtime routine? Your parents? Who and what made you feel safe, loved and secure?

Reflection 2
Take a close look at the nightly steps outlined in FAITH5 below. What jumps out at you?

Step 1:   SHARE your highs and lows.

Step 2:   READ a Bible verse or story.

Step 3:   TALK about how the Bible reading might relate to your highs and lows.

Step 4:   PRAY for one another's highs and lows.

Step 5:   BLESS one another before turning out the lights on the day.

To watch videos on this theme, learn **Psalm 4:8** in song and American Sign Language, and download free weekly devotional resources, go to www.faith5.org/intro.

Which of these enrichuals (faith practices) are you already using in your family? Which would you find most valuable to add at this point to your nightly routine?

Reflection 3
Discuss one of the following:

- *For families with young children:* Look far ahead in time. What would it be worth to you to have a teenager one day who wouldn't go to sleep without talking to you? Praying with you? Blessing you? Would it be worth five minutes? Tonight? Every night?

- *For families with preteens:* What would happen to your family over time if you were able to keep open, caring communication going every night throughout adolescence?

- *For families with teenagers:* How might this type of caring conversation change a family if they were intentional and consistent about it? What might sabotage the effort? Would the benefits outweigh the hassle of trying to invest this time of care, listening and prayer each night in your home? Why or why not?

- *For church leaders and everyone else:* What would happen to a family over time if they made an intentional point of doing FAITH5 most nights? What would happen to your church five years from today if the majority of your households were doing these enrichuals (active listening, Scripture, faith talk, prayer and blessings) nearly every night?

This Week's Challenge

Commit to trying FAITH5 every night before bedtime. Whoever is going to bed first calls "huddle up!" or "FAITH5!" or "highs and lows—five minutes!" and names the room for sharing. Use the free

Introduction Home Huddle Journal download at www.faith5.org/intro/ weekly to record your highs, lows and prayers of the week. If you are living alone, commit to calling a friend or family member every night this week to show you care and to test the process. In addition, you may want to consider:

- Watching me introduce FAITH5 at www.faith5.org/intro/ rich

- Watching Ann and Alan Eustis tell their FAITH5 family story at www.faith5.org/intro/story

- Learning this week's Bible verse, Psalm 4:8, in song and American Sign Language with Christy Smith at www. faith5.org/ intro/song

You can also download weekly resources, nightly Bible verses, videos, games and other free resources at www.faith5.org/intro/ weekly.

Notes

1. Watch the Eustis video at www.faith5.org/intro/story.

2. John J. Ratey, *Spark: The Revolutionary New Science of Exercise and the Brain* (New York: Little, Brown and Company, 2008), p. 38.

3. Faith Inkubators is a Christian education systems think tank and learning organization dedicated to bringing Christ to families and families to Christ every night in every home. Find out more at www.faithink.com.

Share

(Highs and Lows)

Where can I go from your spirit? Or where can I flee from your presence?
If I ascend to heaven, you are there; if I make my bed in Sheol, you are there.
PSALM 139:7-8

The first step toward holding your family together may be the easiest of all if you can but make the time. Step 1 involves simply taking turns sharing your highs and lows at the close of the day.[1] Some call these "pows and wows." President Barack and Michelle Obama call them "roses and thorns." I even have a high-churched pastor friend who calls them "*glorias* and *kyries*" ("praise be" and "Lord, have mercy"). Whatever you call them, model this step for your children by sharing your own highs and lows.

A FAITH5 Family Story

Laura Worthington was asleep when her husband, Matt—a six-foot, four-inch, 280-pound police officer suffering from bipolar disorder—slit her throat and then walked out to the back porch and shot himself.[2] Everyone was stunned and shocked by the terrible power of the disease and the sad

---

To learn **Psalm 139:7-8** in song and American Sign Language, go to www.faith5.org/share/song.

---

days that followed. My good friend Pastor Scott Ness had spoken with Matt a number of times before the incident about how much he loved his two little girls. Laura, who loved her husband deeply, survived the attack and started counseling immediately, but she knew her daughters needed help as well.

"You can't cave," said Laura, who is now a women's self-defense teacher. "You can't wallow in self-pity. You can't let things consume you. When everything happened with me I just thought, *I've got two little girls to deal with*."

Laura has come to see an application of FAITH5 as a dose of nightly therapy for her girls. "My oldest has a constant low, which is, 'Daddy passed away.' At first, especially when it was new, she would get emotional and start to cry. So I would try to bring the positive out of it by saying, 'Okay, but think of all the good things you've got.' Now that [positive input] is part of our nightly routine. That's bedtime. That's what we do. My youngest is just now getting into it at four. It teaches my daughters to be thankful for the good and helps them realize every day isn't perfect—but that's life."

Laura ends each night by tracing a cross on her daughters' foreheads. A few weeks into this, her oldest started blessing her back with a new twist. She now follows the cross symbol every night with the tracing of a heart.

You gotta open the kid before you open the book.
MELHEIMIAN MAXIM #1[3]

Part I: Sharing Highs

Mr. Capote's Advice

You have to set the stage before you raise the curtain. You have to till the soil before you plant the seed. Sharing a high opens the conversation by opening the kid. It also opens communication, hearts, attitudes and doors. But how can you get children into the practice of looking for the good in each day? How can you get them to begin their nightly check-in with a positive memory?

When I was a college student, I volunteered to help run a writers' conference where the Pulitzer Prize-winning author Truman Capote was keynoting. Following the event, the president of the university invited students and faculty who helped with the conference to a reception at his mansion.

Excited to meet the strange little man, I cornered Capote in the den by the baby grand piano and asked a question: "Mr. Capote, how do you become a writer?"

I'll never forget his answer: "You write."

I thought his response was brilliant. I had to run out right away and get a pen to write it down.

One learns to dance by dancing. One learns to paint by painting. One learns to shoot skeet by shooting skeet. One learns to share feelings by sharing feelings. One learns to listen by listening. If you want to raise children into resilient adults who know how to handle any situation life can throw at them, you need to raise children who practice by talking through their highs and lows every night.

The Psychology of Sharing Highs

Starting the night out on a high sets the stage for an overall positive experience. Sharing highs creates a feeling of wellbeing—even regarding what might have seemed to your children to be a terrible, horrible, no good, very bad day. Sharing highs validates both the person and the high: "Yeah, that was pretty neat!" It models healthy communication, engenders caring, fosters acceptance and teaches appreciation.

Sharing the positive triggers even more positive. Sonja Lyubo-mirsky, one of the world's leading researchers on happiness, believes that if you want to develop lifelong satisfaction, you need to engage regularly in positive thinking about yourself, share your happiest events with others, and savor every positive experience in your life.[4]

Peri+Spective

Starting with a positive high reframes the entire day in a healthy and balanced way. Intentionally and consistently sharing the good first changes your outlook (how you see the world), your "in-look" (how you see yourself), and your perspective. The word "perspective" (*peri+spect*) literally means to "look around." So look around. Maybe today wasn't all bad. Look around. Maybe there was some good after all. Look around. If nothing else, you are still alive and, for some odd reason, these people love you. Look around.

There are always flowers for those who want to see them.

HENRI MATISSE

See What You're Looking For

My friend John Lace is an avid hunter and fly fisherman. When we would ride through the countryside, he would often see things I didn't see. "Look, there's a pheasant. Look, there's a bunny. Look, I bet that's a great stream for trout." John was able to find what he wanted to find because he had trained himself to see what he wanted to see.

If you are looking for the bad in a situation, a relationship, a job or a day, you are likely to see it. If you are looking for the good, you are likely to see that, too. Most people do. Train your children to look for the blessings in every day. The persistent practice and pursuit of positive perspective is a marvelous gift you can give to your children, yourself and the great-grandchildren you will never meet. The power of a positive outlook will ripple out like a stone thrown into a pond to bless distant shores.

> A positive attitude may not solve all your problems, but it will annoy enough people to make it worth the effort.
>
> HERM ALBRIGHT

The Sociology of Sharing Highs

A woman once told me in counseling, "I don't like any of my loved ones." I'm guessing there wasn't a lot of joy shared between them. Sociologically, sharing joy, laughter and the positive events of the day creates new bonds and strengthens old ones.

Sharing highs enhances both energy and synergy between you and your mates. It helps shed light on the experienced joys of others, turning mates and inmates into intimates. It gives insight as it gives outsight into what other people's highs are. It deepens understanding about what is important to them. It multiplies affirmation as it builds depth into the relationship.

Multiplying Joy

Some say joy doubles when you share it. I say joy multiplies by the number of people whom you invite in on the sharing. Have you ever gone to a comedy movie alone? Everyone may have praised the film as hilarious, but you watched it alone and, as the credits rolled, you didn't consider it all that funny. However, if you had been with friends, the movie may have been a totally different experience. You would have chuckled and laughed more, ribbed each other and leaned into each other's joy. You might have enjoyed the film twice as much (or more) if only you had shared it with people you already enjoyed.

Attention Intention

The act of active listening is an acknowledgment that the other person is there and a silent statement that he or she matters to you. The gift of one's complete attention affirms the other person and confirms the value of the relationship. It validates both the giver and receiver and tells the receiver that he or she is worth being heard.

Giving the gift of attention is a wonderful way of showing love—sharing love. It creates confidence (*con+fidea* means "with faith") and trust between the sharer and the sharee. One might say it creates "share ease" between the sharees.

A pessimist sees the difficulty in every opportunity; an optimist sees the opportunity in every difficulty.

WINSTON CHURCHILL

Death Eaters and Joy Suckers

Some people suck the joy and life out of the air the moment they enter the room. They live like Eeyore in *Winnie the Pooh*, with a black cloud covering them and everyone they meet. You see them coming and you want to walk the other way. Their negativity, like cheap perfume, arrives before they do and lingers long after they are gone.

Other people make you smile, and you shake your head when thinking of them. My friend Jim Kotz is that way. The first time we met, he was 18 and I was a 23-year-old student pastor. He appeared suddenly in my office like Kramer on Seinfeld, sporting a big Cheshire Cat-grin a mile wide that made me think, *I don't know what he's up to, but I want in on it.* I am smiling right now just thinking of him.

Which kind of person do you want your child to become? A person of joy and smiles, or a person of desperate negative frowns? Which do you want your children to see in you? What are you doing tonight to make your home the kind of place your child and their friends want to be around? People are drawn toward others who make them smile, laugh and enjoy life. So plant positive seeds beginning tonight by sharing your highs. Then nurture, weed and protect those precious seeds as your children grow.

In Galatians 6:7, Paul writes, "Do not be deceived; God is not mocked, for you reap whatever you sow." You reap what you sow. You get what you grow. You will see what you seed.

Guaranteed.

> A man is but the product of his thoughts.
> What he thinks, he becomes.
> MAHATMA GANDHI

The Neurology of Sharing Highs

Neurologically, sharing a high triggers a cascade of positive and powerful neurochemical transmitters that bolster immune systems, regulate hormonal systems, improve one's digestive tract, slows down the aging process, and triggers positive electro-chemical exchanges throughout the brain and the body.

As you recall and relive your highs, a subconscious smile spreads across your face. Your heart may begin to race. Joy and laughter bubble up from inside as an electrical message flows from your brain at 100 yards per second. The memory message speeds down your neurons to the ends of each wire-like cell, where little bags of chemicals are waiting to be released.

There, the electrical message changes to a chemical message and jumps across the space between the neurons (synapses) to bond to proteins on the other side. The electrical message changes to a chemical message, and then back into an electrical message. In an instant, all through your body flashes an electrical/chemical charge that shouts out to every cell, "I feel good!"

What does all this mean?

Free drugs! If you teach your children how to dispense the natural highs our Creator built right into their bodies, maybe they won't need to grab the pills, the bottle or the needle one day when they are feeling down.

Marvelous Exhaustion

Have you ever laughed so hard you could barely breathe? Afterward, you were exhausted, but you felt great! You know what that feeling was?

Free drugs.

I once heard a psychologist on *Good Morning America* say that people ought to stand in front of a mirror every morning and laugh their fool heads off for two straight minutes before heading to work or school. Why? Because the human brain cannot distinguish between fake laughter and real laughter. The result is you still get . . . free drugs!

Don't believe it? Try this. Stare at a mirror (or a friend's face) and laugh as hard as you can for one solid minute. Ready? Go! (1, 2, 3, . . .) When you are through, take three deep cleansing breathes. What happened? You just gave yourself a dose of free drugs! How do you feel?

You feel great.

Imagine your home if laughter and joy filled it every night. Your family would laugh yourselves to health. You would create children who love the nightly interaction with you and yearn to create similar communities of closeness for themselves and their families the rest of their lives.

Imagine a church that shared joys, laughter and highs like this every week in worship. You could put a sign on the parking lot that said, "Come to the church with free drugs." Your attendance would double in a week.

Sharing highs is cleansing, cathartic and beautiful. And it's free.

Medicating Mama

If you have teens, consider this: By sharing your highs, you can medicate your teenagers every night. In the same way, your teenagers can medicate you by sharing their highs. Some nights, don't you think you need it? The wonderful thing about this natural high is that the moment you finish sharing the positive feeling, those chemicals that gave you the high drain back to the original spot on the other side of the neural channel and are ready to fire again. Not just free drugs—but an unlimited supply!

There's a funny thing about parenting teenagers. At about the same time a teen's hormones are kicking in, the parent's hormones are kicking out. (God's got a sense of humor.) I think we all ought to learn how to self-medicate. Every night.

The Theology of Sharing Highs

The Bible calls us repeatedly to share our joy together. The word "rejoice" appears more than 200 times in the Bible. Here are a full week's worth of "rejoice" verses. As you read and consider this list, consider what jumps out to you.

Rejoice with those who rejoice (Rom. 12:15).

You shall rejoice before the Lord your God, you together with your sons and your daughters (Deut. 12:12).

Therefore my heart is glad, and my soul rejoices; my body also rests secure (Ps. 16:9).

Rejoice in the Lord, O you righteous, and give thanks to his holy name! (Ps. 97:12).

This is the day that the Lord has made; let us rejoice and be glad in it (Ps. 118:24).

Rejoice in hope, be patient in suffering, persevere in prayer (Rom. 12:12).

Rejoice in the Lord always; again I will say, Rejoice (Phil. 4:4).

Reclaiming and Reframing

Sharing a high reclaims, renames, re-games and reframes the day as God's good gift. It teaches that life isn't all bad and that, in fact, it contains a lot of good. Sharing a high lifts us to an attitude of gratitude and lowers us to a deeper appreciation for the Giver of all good gifts.

The words "raise" and "praise" aren't all that different. Neither are the words "rise" and "prize." Even in the midst of trouble, sharing a high helps us think about and celebrate the good. It reminds us to praise our God from whom all blessings flow. The reformer Martin Luther said the following about the words "God" and "good":

We Germans from ancient times call God (more elegantly and appropriately than any other language) by that name from the word Good, as being an eternal fountain which gushes forth abundantly nothing but what is good, and from which flows forth all that is and is called good.[5]

God is good—all the time—and sharing highs reminds us of that truth. Sharing them every night surrounded by people who celebrate with us plants seeds of gratitude in our midst and in our minds before we go to sleep. It's not just a good and godly way to grow a grateful child, but it's also a great and godly way to grow a grateful adult.

Part II: Sharing Lows

Creating a Sacred Space

If you only know your child's highs, then you don't know them. If you only know their lows, then you don't know them. And if they don't know their highs and lows, then they don't know themselves either. Simply asking a child, "How was your day?" is rarely enough to solicit more than a vague one-syllable, "Fine."

What do you learn when they say, "Fine"?

Not a lot.

As positive, potent and powerful as it is to start your nightly home huddle with a high, it may be even more important to build the time, place and "sacred space" into your family ritual. What is a sacred space? It is an attitude as much as a place—a moment your children can set aside to invite God into the heart of the matter, feel safe enough to share their lows, and work them out.

The Psychology of Sharing Lows

Sharing lows gives you a better understanding of yourself and others. Growing up with a forum, format and life-long experience in verbalizing one's lows aloud within the context of a safe, loving, non-judgmental home every night gives a child a huge advantage when it comes to building capacity for mental health, emotional re-silience and spiritual maturity.

The Voldemort Effect

There is great power in being able to speak the name of your prob-lems out loud. I call this the "Voldemort Effect," after the evil being in the *Harry Potter* series by J. K. Rowling. No one dared speak his name aloud except Harry.

"He who shall not be named" holds a mysterious and sinister grip on everyone—a hidden power—until the Harry Potters of the world decide, "We are not going to remain silent. We will not cower as captives to fear. We are going to name that sucker out loud. We are going to call him what he is and who he is so that we can deal with the real problem, not the myth. We are going to draw him out into the open, and then kill him together or together die trying!"

A strange and wonderful thing happens the moment you dare speak the name of "he who shall not be named" aloud. A subtle but significant power transfer begins. The moment the silence is bro-ken, the power starts to drain away from its sinister source and move in the direction of those who dare deal with it.

In that moment, if spoken aloud and shared within the confi-dence of a loving family or a trusted family of friends, the newly transferred power begins to grow, strengthen and multiply. There, in the hands and hearts of the people who love you and want the best for you, a treasure trove of solutions, allies, creativity and un-tapped resources suddenly spring to the surface. The Rebel Alliance, the Elves, the Hobbits, the students of Hogwarts and the Narnians are emboldened as they suddenly see that they have a chance.

Okay, too many mixed "narraphors." You get the point. As for Lord Voldemort, let's just say, "Leave him unnamed and he grows each day; name him aloud and he shrinks away."

Light, Sound, Sight and Things that Go Bump in the Night

Another strange and wonderful thing happens the moment the hid-den is revealed aloud. When the unspoken problem is finally brought to light, sound and sight—when the tip of the sliver or the source of the scare is finally exposed—the problem will often appear much less formidable than you originally thought. The shadow on the wall may be no monster at all. The things that go bump in the night might be no more of a fright than a cat, a furnace or a tree branch tapping against the window.

It may be that the boogieman *is* hiding under your bed, but it may be that he's hiding there because he, too, is afraid. The great and powerful Oz may be nothing more than a frightened little man behind a curtain, who is in need of compassion, care and a balloon ride to Kansas. Or the sinister force may actually be Lord Voldemort, and at this very moment he quite possibly may be rallying his forces to kill you. Either way, wouldn't you want to know? Better still, wouldn't you want the people who love you to know?

Life is pain . . . anyone who tells you differently is selling something.
WESLEY, IN *THE PRINCESS BRIDE*

Blisters and Slivers

Some pain is like a blister—leave it alone and it will eventually dry up and fade away. But most pain is like a sliver. It hurts to dig a sliver out, but if you don't get it, then it's going to get you. If you don't get out the sliver—the *whole* sliver—then it will eventually infect you and affect everyone who loves you.

If you are so unaware that you don't even know there is a sliver, then it's even worse. You may live life shaming, naming and blaming everyone else for your own problems, and you'll probably live most of that life alone.

I Feel Your Pain

Have you ever tried to love someone who wouldn't let you into his or her pain? Chances are you found it to be a frustrating experience. It's difficult, if not impossible, to love others in the ways they need to be loved if they can't be honest enough to tell you where and why it hurts.

Maybe they don't trust you. Maybe they don't trust themselves. Maybe they know the source of their pain and won't say. Maybe they've been burned before by naming the problem and are afraid you will judge them. You won't love them. You will leave. Or maybe they don't even know the source of the problem themselves. Either way, a relationship gets stuck in cold, empty silence when slivers remain embedded and problems go unnamed.

Do you know someone who seems to be "fine" on the surface but often explodes? They can be going along at a steady emotional pace for a long while, and then suddenly, and seemingly out of nowhere, bang! They lose it. That's the sign of someone with a deeply embedded sliver; someone who never learned how to dig it out.

To Shrink the Shrink

Society is filled with people who haven't had the forum, format or modeling about how to deal with their problems. We have to pay people to listen to us in this culture. How sad and tragic is that? I am glad there are caring, trained counselors who can help us dig deep, but wouldn't it be cheaper, better and more proactive to raise a generation of children who didn't need to bury their problems in the first place?

Patient: What can I do to cure my problems?
Psychiatrist: Nothing, dear, you're not qualified.

When it comes to stress-related problems, children are at the most risk. The habits and stress-coping mechanisms that parents and caregivers set in place for them early on will follow them the rest of their lives and either bless or curse their world. According to the American Psychological Association's (APA) survey, stress is taking its toll on the young:

Children are hurting. Almost a third of children reported that in the last month they had experienced a physical health symptom often associated with stress, such as headaches, stomachaches or trouble falling or staying asleep. In addition, parents don't realize their own stress is affecting their kids. While 69 percent of parents say their stress has only a slight or no impact on their children, just 14 percent of youth say their parents' stress doesn't bother them. When kids are under stress, she explains, they may eat too much, sleep too much or favor sedentary coping activities like watching television; the resulting weight gain and the teasing and bullying that often accompany it can lead in turn to more stress, creating a cycle that can be difficult to escape from.[6]

According to Norman B. Anderson of the APA, 75 percent of all health-care costs are associated with chronic illnesses, and a key driver of chronic illnesses is stress.[7] In fact, the Centers for Disease Control report that more than half of all deaths between the ages of 1 to 65 result from stress.[8] Another study estimates that 110 million people worldwide lose their lives annually to disease caused by unmanaged stress.[9] Although the United States accounts for only 5 percent of the world's population, we consume 33 percent of all anti-anxiety pills.[10] Stress can be directly linked to all six leading causes of death: heart disease, cancer, lung disease, accidents, cirrhosis of the liver, and suicide.[11]

A good shrink can help you shrink your problems. But why not teach your children how to shrink their own problems while they're young enough and the problems are small enough to be self-shrunk? (Hey, I'm cheap, but wouldn't it save a whole lot of time, grief, pills and money?)

Some say light is the best disinfectant. I'd argue that sound is a pretty great disinfectant as well. Giving your child the gift of your time, complete attention and care—along with the practice of sharing their hurts, fears and concerns out loud each night—is a beautiful and powerful step on the road to mental and emotional health.

Mr. Magoo's Christmas

Back in the days when all my family owned was a black-and-white television, I remember watching Mr. Magoo play Ebenezer Scrooge in a cartoon version of Charles Dickens's *A Christmas Carol*. Dickens described Scrooge as being "lonely as an oyster." In one memorable scene, old Scrooge flew back to his childhood with the Ghost of Christmas Past. They peered into a one-room school where Ebenezer was surprised to spot himself sitting in a corner wearing a dunce cap, singing. I'll never forget the scene or the song:

> *A hand for each hand was planned for the world.*
> *Why don't my fingers reach?*
> *Millions of grains of sand in the world.*
> *Why such a lonely beach?*
> *Where is a voice to answer mine back?*
> *Where are two shoes that click to my clack?*
> *I'm ... all alone ...*
> *In the world.*[12]

That was 50 years ago, and I still remember the tune. I also remember thinking, *No wonder he was such a Scrooge! He grew up feeling all alone in the world!*

As a young father blessed with two babies, I made a promise to myself and God: I refuse to let my children grow up thinking Daddy doesn't have time for them, Mommy doesn't have time for them, or that they are all alone in the world.

In an era of texting, Facebook, email, IM and cell phones, sharing highs and lows is a face-to-face, incarnational embodiment of God's love and care. People feel loved when they feel heard. We can "love them through" their problems.

TIM SEITZ-BROWN

The Sociology of Sharing Lows

Sharing a low with the people you love minimizes the pain. It does so not by minimizing the problem but by taking it off your shoulders and placing it into the arms of those who love and trust you the most. Everyone you "let in" is on your team. Everyone "in the know" who loves you now has antenna up searching for solutions. Everyone who cares is now praying to see answers and working to be the answers to the prayers. Everyone has your back.

Sharing a low breaks down lonely walls. It gives you security, fosters vulnerability, and builds a deeper bond than simply sharing a high. It creates an awareness of what is going on in your own inner life and in the inner lives of others. It draws out deep compassion, builds stronger connections, and creates more resilient communities. It allows those you allow inside to know and love you in the ways you yearn to be known and loved. It also allows them to enter creatively, yet more objectively, into your situation, your pain and your prayers. The sharing and the caring that surround the hurt open up the possibility for confession, absolution, forgiveness and reconciliation.

Burning on Entry

The space shuttle was built with ceramic tiles designed to spread the heat of re-entry nose to tail across the entire body of the craft. Without such a design, the heat on the nose of the vehicle would have been so intense that the craft might have exploded. With the heat spread out, however, the danger was manageable.

You likewise have the chance to model and teach your children how to survive even the hottest challenges. Sharing lows with those you love is like spreading the heat around. It's still hot. It still hurts. It's still potentially dangerous. But it's all the more manageable when you are not trying to handle it alone.

- -

 We get better together. We don't get better alone.
RICK WARREN

- -

Cutting the Lows in Fractions

Some say sharing a low cuts the low in half. I say it cuts it into fractions, depending on how many other people know the low, care about you, and are willing to help. If you let just one other person into your pain, you at least will have someone with whom you can complain. You cut it in half. But if there are three people in on the low, it might cut the pain in thirds. If there are 10, you may be able to dilute the pain by a factor of 10.

For Sharing Out Loud

The brilliance and beauty of Alcoholics Anonymous starts with the first step: owning up to your problems and naming them aloud in front of a trusted group of friends. Until that first step happens, no growth, no progress and no healing can begin. You are all alone in the world. Whatever your problem is, if you can simply state it out loud—"Hello, I'm Richard, and I'm a Lutheran"—you are on the royal road to recovery. The power moves toward you and away from the problem. The sliver can be extracted. The ointment can be applied. The healing can begin. If you don't get real, you cannot deal. If you cannot deal, you will not heal. Period.

Sanctuary Much, Ladies and Gentlemen

Sharing lows each night gives your children both the tools and the experience of practicing healthy problem-solving skills in the safe context of loving relationships and a trusting family. This isn't about interference, judgment or intrusion. It's about modeling and practicing active listening, reflection, self-awareness and healthy, caring communication every night.

If you don't take the trash out from time to time, it really starts to stink.
MELHEIMIAN MAXIM #26

These simple practices teach children they don't have to hold anything inside. They are not alone. There are people, places and sacred spaces to get real, to deal and to heal. A home that instills and installs this nightly sharing of both highs and lows becomes a safe sanctuary where tears, fears and even failures can be discussed and worked out in confidence and love. The home becomes a grace place where children can be honest in expressing grief, hurts and disappointments.

This simple and intentional faith practice spins a protective cocoon around a child's fragile development one strand at a time. One low at a time. One night at a time.

Focusing Away from Self

Actively listening to each other's lows allows the listener for a moment to focus on something other than his or her own pain. Imagine raising a teenager who thinks, *Hmmm . . . my mom has problems too,* or, *Hmmm . . . my dad . . . he's a human being.*

Taking turns sharing highs and lows draws you to focus both on yourself and on the needs of others. When you take turns sharing both highs and lows, it teaches you that it's not all about you. (Yes, it is about you—but it's not *all* about you.)

Look Around and Look Again

We mentioned earlier that *peri+spect* means to look around. *Re+spect* means to look again. Sharing a low and listening to others open up and own up to their pain leads to both broader perspective and deeper respect. So look around and look again. Other people have problems, too. Look around and look again. Some of their problems are actually worse than yours, and yet they seem to be coping. Look around and look again. It may be by leaving your pity-party and helping others that you will actually help yourself.

The Neurology of Sharing Lows

What happens neurologically when you share a low? Like sharing a high, a message comes from the brain at 100 yards per second. It speeds down the ends of the neurons. Little bags of neurotransmitter chemicals—amino peptides and endorphins—are released, and they jump across the synapse and bond to a protein on the other side. All through your body, at 100 yards per second, flashes a painkiller!

More free drugs!

When you cry and release the pain, the chemical composition in your tears has a higher concentration of dopamine than do your tears when you laugh. Dopamine is a pleasure enhancer and painkiller. A good cry is powerful medicine! Crying also releases tension, cleanses toxic stress hormones from the body, and increases the body's ability to heal. Not bad side effects for a drug that is free and self-dispensable.

Have you ever cried so hard you were exhausted? Afterward, you felt great. Why wouldn't you give those same free drugs—God's good medicine—every night to the people you love?

Dealing and Healing
Holding negative feelings inside and living with resentment actually hurt the holder more than the "holdee." It raises blood pressure, eats away at the lining of the stomach, erodes the immune system, and sets the holder up for a host of maladies. "I'm so angry at you, I'll get migraines, ulcers and hemorrhoids! That'll show you!" Doesn't make much sense, does it? Yet that is exactly what many of us do by stuffing our pain inside. Brain and spirituality researchers Dr. Andrew Newberg and Mark Waldman write:

> Repressing negative feelings can be damaging, because unconscious anger—and the constant flow of stress hormones and neurochemicals it releases—can literally eat you alive, damaging the emotional-regulation centers of the brain. Research shows that the best way to deal with negativity is to observe it inwardly, without reaction and without judgment. The next step is to consciously reframe each negative feeling and thought by shaping it into a positive, compassionate, and solution-based direction.[13]

Building an Empathetic Brain
Like muscles, whatever areas of the brain you exercise will grow both in strength and capacity over time. As your children practice sharing feelings out loud and learn to listen to the feelings of those around them, they literally grow more brain tissue in the areas that

process sympathy, empathy, compassion and deep care. Sharing a low literally rewires your child's brain.

"It's not just repeated physical actions that can rewire our brains," writes Nicholas Carr in *The Shallows: What the Internet Is Doing to Our Brains*. "Purely mental activity can also alter our neural circuitry, sometimes in far-reaching ways."[14] Carr also notes:

> The mind can essentially train itself to be healthy. It can train itself to be sick. The more a sufferer concentrates on his symptoms, the deeper those symptoms are etched into his neural circuits. . . . Although the use of any kind of tool can influence our thoughts and perspectives—the plow changed the outlook of the farmer, the microscope opened new worlds of mental exploration for the scientist—it is our intellectual technologies that have the greatest and most lasting power over what and how we think.[15]

Sharing lows is an intellectual technology you have at your disposal. Use it nightly and you enlarge the capacity for empathy in your child's brain. You will also turn your home into the kind of grace place that teaches, models and lives healing love every night.

Don't go to bed mad. Stay up and fight.
PHYLLIS DILLER

Stay Up and Fight

Sharing both highs and lows teaches people how to forgive. It builds empathy (*em+pathos*, meaning "in pain"), sympathy (*sym+pathos*, meaning "with pain"), compassion (*com+passion*, meaning "suffering along with") and camaraderie. It validates, affirms and strengthens the other person. It creates (commiserates) people who enter each other's pain willingly to share it and bear it with them, rather than people who are dragged into another's pain kicking and screaming and trying their best to get away from them. Sharing lows builds all these gifts and all that support into the core of the family ritual. Why would you *not* want to give these gifts to your child tonight and every night?

A Word of Caution: The Tired or Sensitive Child

Be sure to give each low its time, but don't dwell on any one low for too long. Some children, if they are particularly tired and sensitive, may not be able to move beyond their lows to experience the help that God and your family are offering to them. Kaitlyn Jenkins, a youth and family ministry director at her church in eastern Ohio, has been doing highs and lows for years with her children. This former biology and English teacher-turned-mother-turned-youth-specialist offers a word of warning:

> We had to stop doing "lows" in our house for a season until we figured out some stuff. My son at age 9 sunk into a little depression during FAITH5 when it was time to remember the low of the day. We could even see the transition on his face as he went from high to low, and then slowly spiral down into the low. He went to bed in tears not long after we started. We'd talk, pray, reassure, comfort and feel helpless. Night after night it was the same low and the same drop. After much frustration, we finally figured out that he was tired at the end of the day, and his low seemed so overwhelming to his tired little brain that he fell apart. When he experienced so much emotion around the same issue every night, he assumed it was a big problem he couldn't fix, and it just got bigger. So, we've done a couple of things: First, I started to ask him his highs and lows in an earlier part of the day. Second, we now call our highs "shining stars" and our lows "silver linings." We share lows with the intent of looking for some good God might be bringing out of the bad situation. Third, we share silver linings so that we can finish on a high.

Now that the kids have gotten older, Carrie says things have settled down a bit. They do FAITH5 every night at 9:00 PM exactly. "It's a fun race to the finish as the kids run around the house to make it on the couch exactly three seconds before 9:01!"

Newspaper Woes as Personal Lows

On nights when your child can't think of a personal low, you might want to bring a newspaper or magazine into your sharing time. Challenge your children to look outside themselves a moment. Look around and look again (*peri+spect* and *re+spect*). You don't need to flip too far into the paper to realize that there are millions of children around the world who are starving, without homes, and trapped in poverty.

Look around and look again. There is a world of pain, a world in need, and a world of insatiable greed. Look around and look again. Maybe God is calling your child to be part of the solution with his or her life rather than part of the problem. Look around and look again. That child in the newspaper doesn't have shoes on his or her feet or a bed to sleep in, and here your children are complaining about having to shop at Walmart for school clothes or drive an old car to school! Look around and look again, this time with the eyes of Christ.

The experience of bringing a newspaper into the nightly ritual can grow a self-centered, inward-turning child into a young adult who is both aware and filled with such care that he actually does something for this hurting world with his life.

A Theology of Sharing Lows

The Bible calls us again and again to place our problems before one another and God for mutual care and support during hard times. The following is a week's worth of nightly compassion Scriptures. As you read and consider this list, what jumps out?

Weep with those who weep (Rom. 12:5).

Bear one another's burdens, and in this way you will fulfill the law of Christ (Gal. 6:2).

And be kind to one another, tenderhearted (Eph. 4:32).

Let each of you look not to your own interests, but to the interests of others (Phil. 2:4).

Therefore encourage one another and build up each other, as indeed you are doing (1 Thess. 5:11).

Come to me, all you that are weary and are carrying heavy burdens, and I will give you rest (Matt. 11:28).

Cast all your anxiety on him, because he cares for you (1 Pet. 5:7).

Sharing lows teaches your children that they are part of life. Sharing these lows before God and a trusted Christian family or a "family of friends" shows your children that they are never alone. Admitting disappointment, weakness, fear and anger out loud is what healthy people do. It reinforces the Church at its most elemental level.

Bigger than Our Biggest Problems

Admitting lows before God and each other will show your family that God is bigger than their biggest complaints, bigger than their biggest problems, and bigger than their biggest questions. It will show your children that it is okay to verbalize what is on their hearts. It teaches them to hang on and wrestle with God and God's people when answers aren't apparent and pain is unrelenting.

Sharing lows in the context of your primary faith community—your family—will give your child experience in looking for and leaning toward God and God's people, especially in the midst of problems. It teaches them how to get real, to deal and to heal. It also calls Christ into the center of the problem, discussion and solution. As Jesus said, "For where two or three are gathered in my name, I am there among them" (Matt. 18:20).

Part III: Highs and Lows for Belles and Beaus

The Differences Between Boys and Girls

I need to say a word about the differences between boys and girls when it comes to sharing highs and lows. According to Dr. Louann Brizendine in *The Female Brain*, little girls are born with 11 percent more brain tissue that is dedicated to speaking and listening than little boys.[16] Little boys are born with two and a half times more brain tissue dedicated to sex drive, plus larger areas of the brain are connected to action and aggression. That's one more reason for a pillow fight before you try to talk! If you don't turn part of your learning process into action up front, your boys will turn it into aggression later on. Take your pick.

The Bad News

According to Dr. Brizendine, the average female speaks approximately 20,000 words each day. In a 16-hour waking day, that equals about 10 minutes per hour. The average male speaks about three and a half minutes per hour, or just 7,000 words in a day. This news is neither good nor bad; it's just the way it is. Expect your son to share—just don't expect him to share as much!

Most nights in the Melheim home, Kathryn Elizabeth would share her highs and lows for 20 minutes once we got her started. Joseph Martin would generally "get it over with" in three seconds using three or four syllables: "school's stupid" and "almost Friday." Most girls actually enjoy talking more than most boys. It's a matter of chemistry. According to the Woman's Passion website:

> The simple speech act causes emission of hormones in a woman's brain, giving her the same sensations which a drug addict feels after he receives a long-awaited dose. Differences between male and female brains are already formed in a mother's womb, when testosterone starts af-

fecting formation of the developing male brain. As a result of this influence, zones controlling speech, emotions and memory in a man's brain decrease. Thus, boys, and later men, speak less than women and try to hide their emotions as much as they can.[17]

I have no clinical evidence, but I suspect too much talking—if forced—has just the opposite effect on the male brain. In my experience, rather than producing pleasure hormones, forcing a lot of talk out of a boy who isn't in the mood might actually produce stress hormones.

The Good News

That's the bad news. The good news is that the brain, like any muscle, grows in the areas in which it is exercised most. So, if you want to grow a little boy into a young man who will express his thoughts and feelings to you, his future spouse and his future kids, you need to start today.

Set the stage for open and caring communication. Model it with both sexes. Try your best to practice compassionate communication. The more you talk now, the more you will enlarge your boy's capacity to talk later. Just because you aren't hearing major significant lows coming out of your son's mouth every night doesn't mean his brain isn't growing. The very act of listening will help your son's brain grow more capacity in the linguistic and phonics areas. Listening will also expand his capacity for emotional depth and care.

Here's the other good news: The standard male communication mode that limits lows to a couple sentences spoken in 10 to 20 seconds may not only be more *efficient* but has also been proven to be significantly more *effective* in getting messages across! Any one-way communication beyond a half-minute increases the likelihood that the message a person is trying to get across will not be registered and remembered by anyone. According to brain and spirituality researchers Dr. Andrew Newberg and Mark Waldman in *Words Can Change Your Brain,* the listener's brain can only recall about 10 seconds of content. Beyond that, nothing is going to register. As Newberg and Waldman write:

> If you talk for several minutes, the other person's brain will only recall a fraction of what you've said, and it might not be the part you want to convey. The solution? Brevity followed by intense listening to make sure the other person has grasped the key points of what you said. If they have, great! You can say another sentence. If not, why move on? If the other person hasn't understood you, what good will it do?[18]

You can keep pouring water in a full glass all you want, but it's only going to hold so much. Everything else will just be a waste of water. Likewise, after 10 seconds, you can keep talking all you want, but if there is no give and take—no true conversation—everything else is just a waste of time, energy and breath.

Aunt Amy's Awesome Advice

My children's brilliant Aunt Amy Kippen runs a cross-generational Sunday and Wednesday school at a church in West Fargo, North Dakota, where 71 percent of the dads are in church with their kids every week.[19]

You heard it right: 71 percent.

Amy considers the hour spent at church each week as the kick-off for the *real* Christian education in her church—the nightly FAITH5 Home Huddles. Eighty-seven percent of the Christian education in her church is done off-site every night. Eighty-seven percent of the prayer ministry happens in homes. Eighty-seven percent of the pastoral care, Bible study and fellowship is done in the most natural small-group ministry of all: the home. Amy doesn't have to recruit a single Sunday School teacher, because every household in her church has its own equipped and motivated guide: a parent.

When it comes to highs and lows, Amy teaches parents not to worry about nights when the sharing seems shallow or insignificant. "Let them share," she says. "No comments. No judgments. If they don't come to you with the insignificant, they will never come to you with the significant. If they don't come to you with nothing, they will never come to you with something."

In our home, seven out of eight nights Joseph Martin's lows were seemingly insignificant. But on the nights when something major, bad or painful had happened, we had the forum and the format in place to draw out the slivers before they could get infected. "I had a problem at school" or "my friend is moving away" or "something bad happened" are all healthy things to say and hear. The importance of sharing lows—especially with a less-verbal boy—is that you are providing a safe space, a true sanctuary, and a healthy enriching ritual that grows mental, emotional and spiritual capacity one night at a time.

The 20-Percent Marriage Insurance Policy

Sharing highs and lows isn't healthy just for kids—journaling highs and lows followed by sharing thoughts out loud is also great for marriages. According to Richard Wiseman in *59 Seconds: Think a Little, Change a Lot,* "Partners who spend a few moments each week committing their deepest thoughts and feelings about their relationship to paper boost their chances that they will stick together by more than 20 percent. Such 'expressive writing' results in partners using more positive language when they speak to each other, leading to a healthier and happier relationship."[20]

Setting aside 5 to 15 minutes each night for these communication practices might not merely hold a family together; it might also teach children—and adults—how to hold a marriage together.

Life moves pretty fast. If you don't stop and look around once in a while, you could miss it.
FERRIS BUEHLER, IN *FERRIS BUEHLER'S DAY OFF*

Home Huddle: How to Start

If all you had time for each night was five minutes of sharing highs and lows, you would be miles ahead of most families—psychologically, sociologically, neurologically and theologically. But this is just the start of the art. In the chapters that follow, we'll get to the good stuff. In the meantime, let's look at how this first step of FAITH5 might look in your nightly routine.

Calling the Huddle

Whoever is going to bed first in your home is empowered to call the nightly home huddle. This could be, "Highs and lows!" or "Huddle up!" or "FAITH5 in five minutes!" After a little exercise to get oxygen, glucose and BDNF coursing through your children's veins, invite each person to look back on the day. What was one high (a good thing) that happened during the last 24 hours? What was one low (one thing they didn't consider so great)?

Go around the room. Take turns. Ask everyone to be on watch throughout the day for the highest high and the lowest low. Consider recording your highs and lows in a journal for later reflection. Think of this as a little gift to your family and yourself. Be honest. Be real. Don't interrupt. Expect everyone to contribute.

Rotating Rooms

Some people have a dedicated space where the sharing of highs and lows always takes place. Others allow the first person going to bed to convene the meeting and call the space. "My room! Five minutes!"

When our children were young, our pillow fight always ended on our waterbed. We followed with highs and lows on the waves. When they hit grade school, the home huddle rotated between Kathryn's and Joseph's rooms. For some magical unseen reason, it shifted back to Mom and Dad's bedroom when they hit high school.

Most nights found them lying comfortably on our bed—often with Kathryn Elizabeth's feet sticking in my face for a foot rub. Even on nights when we were angry with one another and not all that elated to be related, the act of returning to that ritual and comforting space was often all it took to bring us back "home" in our home.

Two Rules

We only had two rules for sharing highs and lows when our children were young. First, no interruptions. When someone was sharing, no one else was allowed to speak, except to ask clarifying questions. Second, no judgment. The first time you judge your children's highs or lows may be the last time they risk being honest with you about what is really going on in their lives.

Three Tools

With the hindsight of a nostalgic empty-nester and the insight of a lot more reading in neurology since my children were babies, I now know of three tools I wish I had used in the Melheim home while they were young. These are:

1. *A timer.* Brevity is the way to go for highs and lows, so set a time limit for the amount of sharing. Save the longer conversation for Step 3: Talk.

2. *Journaling:* Writing before speaking is brilliant neurology. It connects thought to muscles, motions to emotions, and eyes to fingers. It begins the process of moving a person's short-term memory from scratch pad (hippocampus) to hard drive (neo cortex). Writing connects the brain to the body to the environment, thus engaging the whole mind. It wires and fires and connects the new to what you already knew, setting the pieces in place for insight, problem-solving and innovation. If you want to grow reflective children into wise and thankful adults, start journaling.

3. *Photographs and "emotographs":* As long as you are journaling words, why not consider adding a journal of images? Take at least one photo every day and add it to the mix. Mental and emotional snapshots recorded in the form of simple sentences about your highs, lows and prayers serve as great mementos. Add a photo each day along

with your writing and your journal will become the kind of scrapbook I call an emotograph—a rich, simple, memory-jogging tool that ensures that the day and its lessons will never be forgotten.

Absent Parents

What if you frequently have to go out of town on business? What if you are sitting on a military base half a world away? What if you are sitting in a jail or prison cell? All the more reason to connect with your kids! Your kids need you now more than ever in order to feel loved, secure and safe.

Do everything in your power to check in regularly with your kids, ask about their highs and lows, share your own concerns, pray for them, ask for their prayers, and offer your blessing. Don't let physical distance create emotional distance. Let them know that even though you are away, you care too much about them to let a single day go by without building a memory they will treasure and take with them the rest of their lives. They will remember that their daddy or mommy always had time for them.

You can't buy that kind of message for a child. It will mean more to him or her than you will ever know.

Dream Team Reflections

Where can I go from your spirit?
Or where can I flee from your presence?
If I ascend to heaven, you are there;
if I make my bed in Sheol, you are there.
PSALM 139:7

Gather with your family, friends or a small group of people you trust and respect to share the following.

To watch videos on this theme, learn **Psalm 139:7** in song and American Sign Language, and download free weekly devotional resources, go to www.faith5.org/share.

Theme Verse

Read and highlight today's theme verse in your Bible, and then hop online to the link below to learn this verse in song and American Sign Language.

Reflection 1

Think of your highest high and lowest low in the last five years.

- Where was God in the high?
- Where was God in the low?
- What wisdom have you gained from these two experiences?

Reflection 2

Put on your psychologist's hat for a moment. What happens to a person when he or she:

- Shares a significant high with a trusted friend?
- Shares a significant low with a trusted friend?
- Falls asleep every night of his or her life knowing that he or she is loved, heard and valued?

Reflection 3

Put on your sociologist's hat for a moment. What happens to a family when they:

- Reflect on the significant highs of the day every night?
- Reflect on the significant lows of the day every night?
- Share highs and lows, caring conversations, faith talk and reflection at the end of the day (as opposed to mornings, after school, in the car or around the dinner table)?

This Week's Challenge

Commit to trying just the first step of FAITH5 every night before bedtime this week. Whoever is going to bed first calls "huddle up!" or "FAITH5!" or "highs and lows—five minutes!" and names the room for sharing. Use the free Share Home Huddle Journal download at www.faith5.org/share/weekly to record your highs and lows. If you are living alone, commit to calling a friend or family member every night this week and asking them to share their highs and lows. Come back next time ready to share your experience. In addition, you may want to consider:

- Watching me discuss sharing highs and lows at www.faith5 .org/share/rich

- Watching Laura Worthington tell her FAITH5 family story at www.faith5.org/share/story

- Learning this week's Bible verse, Psalm 139:7, in song and American Sign Language with Christy Smith at www.faith5 .org/share/song

You can also download weekly resources, nightly Bible verses, videos, games and other free resources at www.faith5.org/share/ weekly.

Read

Your word is a lamp to my feet and a light to my path.
PSALM 119:105

The second step toward holding your family together is to read a key Bible verse or story with your family each night.

A FAITH5 Family Story

Benny Gillund has autism. If his parents, Brent and Brenda Jo, and sister, Tacy, forget to drag out their Bibles and do FAITH5, he reminds them. "One of the best things about FAITH5 is that it's a routine for Ben," says Brent. "He does a lot better with routine. We've incorporated it, and it's now second nature to him."

"It's one of the best things that has ever happened to us," says Brenda Jo. "It encourages good communication. It is a priority every day. And it's not just dad-led; it is family-led. If we forget to do it, the kids remind us. It's just a wonderful opportunity to keep us together as a family and keep God at the center."[1]

To learn **Psalm 119:105** in song and American Sign Language, go to www.faith5.org/read/song.

Part I: What Are We Feeding Our Children?

Sawdust and Manure

Why is it so important to fill our children's hearts and minds with the wisdom, will and wonder of the Word of God? The reason is because if we don't fill them with the good stuff, the world will fill them with something much less by default. A story from the Second World War illustrates this point.

During the 872-day siege of Leningrad (from 1941 to 1944), the city elders had a difficult decision to make. The Nazis had cut off most supply routes to the city, and the few remaining truck routes across the frozen lake were being bombed daily. By the fall of 1941, it became clear there was only one-third enough grain to get the city through the winter. By November, 350 people were dying daily. By December, 1,600 corpses were turning up on the streets each day.

What would the elders do? Would they cordon off two-thirds of the city and feed only one-third? They couldn't bear to make that decision, so instead they mixed their bread with anything they could find—sawdust, cottonseed, cellulose and manure.[2] That winter, hundreds of thousands of children went to bed starving to death on bloated stomachs. When the siege finally lifted, somewhere between 635,000 and one million Russians had perished in that city alone.

Most parents want the best for their children, but what are we feeding them?

Completely Full, Yet Completely Empty

As parents, most of us want only the best for our children. We would do anything, give anything and sacrifice everything if our children were sick or in danger. That is the crazy nature of a parent's love.

Most mothers go up two dress sizes and turn prematurely gray for their children. They are invested! Most fathers would jump in front of a speeding truck for their children without thinking twice.

That's the kind of love they possess. Parents sweat, slave, give, forgive and then give some more without a word of thanks. Most would still take a bullet for their children even on those days when their children yell and slam the door, saying, "I hate you! I never want to speak to you again! Can I have a ride to the mall?"

Parents are crazy. They are crazy in love. They are crazy committed. And today, most are crazy afraid—afraid their children will walk away physically, emotionally or spiritually. For Christian parents, any one of these three would tear their hearts out of their chest. That's how much they love their kids. Those who once carried a baby forever carry a mystical, unexplainable bond in their hearts.

Yet these same Christian parents often never stop to consider what they are feeding their children. As I mentioned previously, I have spent the last 35 years focused on youth and family ministries. I have worked with thousands of churches, tens of thousands of pastors and youth workers, and hundreds of thousands of children, youth and families on four continents. During that time, I have come to observe something that haunts me. When it comes to our first-world lifestyle, we have a lot of full houses and empty homes. We have full schedules and empty lives. We have the Bread of Life readily available, but we are feeding our children a steady diet of mental sawdust and spiritual manure.

None of us in our right mind would let our children pick up something off the street and put it in their mouths if we had something nourishing to feed them. Yet with televisions blaring mindlessly in the background and smartphones and iPads pulsing endlessly in the foreground, we are allowing our children to pick up anything and everything that comes over the air. Every sexual image and off-color joke. Every Viagra commercial. Every hero that blows away the villains while taking a drag on a cigarette. Every program that makes dads look like mindless idiots, moms look like overbearing control freaks, and Christians look like judgmental, gay-bashing characters on *Good Christian Belles*.[3]

We are completely full, and yet we are completely empty. We have no time for the best because we settle for the rest. Even worse, we allow our children to drift off to sleep with the most convenient and mindless mental bedtime snacks available, with the television and Internet serving up a super-sized, steady diet of—you guessed it—sawdust and manure.

Making the decision to have a child is momentous. It is to decide forever to have your heart go walking around outside your body.
ELIZABETH STONE

The Mass, the Mess, the Message and the Massage

Let me tell you what kind of competition the Christian "meal plan" is up against these days. According to research collected by my brilliant friend Dr. Ted Baehr and the staff at Movie Guide, by the time a child growing up today reaches the age of 18, he or she will be exposed to 60,000 hours of media, 11,000 hours of school, and a mere 2,000 hours in quality conversations with his or her parents.

A study titled "The M2 Generation: Are Your Kids Too Dependent on the Media?" suggests that American children are spending 7.5 hours per day (52.5 hours a week) with all forms of media.[4] Because multiple devices are often playing at the same time, total media exposure rises to 10.75 hours per day (76 hours per week). *What are our children's minds "eating" and absorbing during this uncensored screen and media time?*

- The average American child hears 38 sexual references each day and 14,000 each year.[5]
- That child will have seen 8,000 murders on TV by age 12.[6]
- By age 18, he or she will have seen 200,000 violent acts and 16,000 murders.[7]
- Two-thirds of all programming contains violence.[8]
- Programs designed for children more often contain violence than do programs for adults on TV.[9]

- Most violent acts go unpunished on TV and are often accompanied by humor. The consequences of human suffering and loss are rarely depicted.[10]
- Many shows glamorize violence. TV often promotes violent acts as a fun and effective way to get what you want without consequences.[11]
- Even in G-rated animated movies, violence is common. Often, it is depicted as a way for the good characters to solve their problems.[12]
- Children imitate the violence they see on TV. Children under age 8 often cannot tell the difference between reality and fantasy, making them more vulnerable to learning from the violence they see on TV and adopting it as reality.[13]
- Even "good guys" beating up "bad guys" gives a message that violence is normal and okay. Many children will try to be like their good-guy heroes during their playtimes.[14]
- A University of Michigan researcher demonstrated that watching violent media can reduce a child's willingness to help others in need.[15]
- A 17-year-long study found that teenaged boys who grew up watching a lot of TV each day are more likely to commit acts of violence than those who watched less.[16]
- Merely having a TV on in the home is linked to more aggressive behavior in three-year-olds. This is regardless of the type of programming and regardless of whether the child is actually watching the show.[17]

According to a University of Michigan health system study of American households:

- Two-thirds say TV is "usually on" during meals.
- 51 percent of respondents admit TV is on most waking hours, whether anyone is watching it or not.
- 53 percent have no rules about watching TV.
- 71 percent of 8- to 18-year-olds have a TV set in their room.[18]

So, who is the more influential teacher today? From the stand-point of raw time, the answer seems pretty clear.

Commercial Non-Breaks

Along with media exposure, perhaps the next most intrusive, annoying and insulting assault on our brains and budgets is the constant barrage of commercial messages we face today. Personal fulfillment, economic riches, popularity, sexual prowess—you name it, it's available in a bottle, a can, an investment strategy or a pill. From the moment the alarm goes off in the morning to the exhausted minutes before our heads hit the pillow and we drift off to sleep, we are bombarded by noise, commercials, noise, messages, noise, sales pitches, noise, stories and the least-common-denominator of the current culture's excuse for humor.

It's hard to get a solid number on how many commercials people are exposed to each day. Statistics range from 1,500 to 5,000, up from 500 in the 1970s.[19] That's somewhere between 547,500 to 1,825,000 per year and 9,855,000 to 32,850,000 by the time a person graduates from high school. Whatever the numbers, one doesn't have to spend a lot of time surfing the Internet, browsing magazines or walking through any city, town or hamlet on the globe without becoming instantly aware that people are being pitched a set of promises that can't possibly be true.

Technophilia

Sherry Turkle, founder and director of MIT's Initiative on Technology and Self, makes a number of critical observations about teens, talk and today's technology:

- Young people are avoiding phone conversations. They don't like to deal with people "in person."[20]
- Young people might be with you, but they are always somewhere else as well.[21]
- We tend the Internet, and the Internet teaches us to need it.[22]

As Turkel explains, "Connectivity becomes a craving: when we receive a text or an email, our nervous system responds by giving us a shot of dopamine—the pleasure drug. We are stimulated by connectivity itself. We learn to require it, even as it depletes us."[23] In his blog *The Technium,* Kevin Kelly—an editor for *Wired,* tech guru and social critic—tells of a teenage girl who literally went through withdrawal when her parents took her mobile phone away:

> An acquaintance of mine has a teenage daughter. Like most teens in this century she spends her day texting her friends, abbreviating her life into 140 character hints, flinging these haikus out to an invisible clan of mutual texters. It's an always-on job, this endless encapsulation of the moment. During dinner, while walking, on the toilet, lounging in bed, or in any state of wakefulness, to chat is to live. Like all teens, my friend's daughter tested the limits of her parents' restrictions. For some infraction or another, they grounded her. And to reinforce the seriousness of her misconduct, they took away her mobile phone. Immediately the girl became physically sick. Faint, nauseous, and so ill she couldn't get out of bed. It was as if her parents had amputated a limb. And in a way they had. Our creations are now inseparable from us. Our identity with technology runs deep, to our core.[24]

Media Effects on Girls

So, what are the results of all this media on young girls? One can speculate, but obesity, depression, neurosis, anti-social behavior, bullying, suicide and low self-esteem in girls are at epidemic proportions. A study commissioned by Dove found that 77 percent of girls between 10 and 14 in the United States and Great Britain describe themselves in negative terms.[25] Many consider themselves fat, ugly and undesirable when they see ads on television and billboards. Ninety percent of women want to change at least one aspect of their appearance. Eighty-one percent of 10-year-olds are afraid of being fat. Only 2 percent of women think they are beautiful.[26] Where does this all lead? Twenty-two percent of American girls seriously consider suicide.[27]

Media Effects on Boys

The results are similar for boys. Twenty-five years ago, 15 percent of Western men were unhappy with their bodies; today, 45 percent are unhappy.[28] Although twice as many girls consider suicide in the United States, twice as many boys complete the act.

Even with all of the social pressures girls appear to be under, at school it appears trouble has shifted sex. ADD, ADHD, dyslexia and a host of related learning difficulties are now an epidemic among boys. For every 100 girls with learning disabilities, there are 276 boys. Not only that, but for every 100 women graduating college, there are 77 men.[29] At some colleges, there are three female coeds for every male student.

Among young men, attitudes toward sex, violence against women, acceptance of recreational and illegal drugs, and a host of other socially detrimental problems are on the rise. Videogame and porn addictions are considered the acceptable norm. The costs are astronomical—mentally, financially, socially, culturally and spiritually. Worse, overwhelming data indicates that we've only seen the tip of the iceberg.

Inescapable

Cell phones ring and texts buzz at all hours of the day and night, connecting us to work, to friends, and to the inescapable busyness and business of post-modern life.

Our iPads, smartphones and laptops with Wi-Fi connections call us awake and follow us back home to sleep, nagging us to type one more text, finish one last post, check our messages one last time "just in case," and finish the work that we didn't get to during the nearly extinct 9-to-5 work day of our parents' era. Then we doze off to a restless sleep and wake up the next day to partake of it all over again.

All the while, we sense a gnawing emptiness while the fresh, steaming nutritious loaf sits in the wrapper on the counter, unopened. "I am the bread of life," says Jesus (John 6:35). And we don't even nibble. We're too full.

Sawdust and manure.

Running on Empty

It's one thing to starve yourself; it's quite another to starve your children. Not that we're physically starving. The most recent CDC statistics show that 33 percent of children are overweight and 17 percent are obese.[30] Over-indulgent, "never say no" parents are happy to fill their little darlings with Skittles and Mountain Dew but are inadvertently setting them up for a life of physical, mental, emotional and spiritual pain. We're happy to fill them full of sugar and carbs and their rooms with computers, flat screens, iPods and the latest video games. I've heard of parents who buy and pay monthly smartphone bills for kids who won't answer when they call, and who pay for cars, gas and insurance for teens who won't take them to Target to get a prescription filled.

We're happy to indulge our children. We fill their schedules with traveling, sports and private lessons; their teeth with ortho-dontia; and their closets with a dizzying array of tech toys to keep them busy from dawn to dusk. Our children's lives are completely full, yet in many ways, many are completely and chronically empty. There is no time for a family meal, let alone a devotional life. Even in the most dedicated Christian homes, there is virtually not even five minutes set aside and available in the day for God's Word, faith talk or prayer.

There is no room in the inn, which in this post-modern era has been turned into a 24-7 iMax multiplex with a casino and an all-you-can-eat buffet on the side. It's booked from now until never. Yet as the disciples said to Jesus, "Lord . . . you have the words of eternal life" (John 6:68).

Alarmist?

Perhaps this sounds as if I am being an alarmist. After all, there have been problems and complaints about teens from the begin-ning of time. Just consider two examples:

Our earth is degenerate in these latter days, bribery and corruption are common, children no longer obey their parents; everyone wants to write a book! (4,700-year-old Assyrian Tablet)

Our youth today love luxury. They have bad manners, contempt for authority, disrespect for older people. Children nowadays are tyrants. They contradict their parents, gobble their food, and tyrannize their teachers. (Socrates, 425 BC)

We have had these problems forever. People thought the written word, then the radio, then television would destroy our culture. Yet here we are, right? How can something as harmless and inane as a television show, a computer game or a smartphone damage a child's future? How can a song on their iPod, a movie watched repeatedly, a video game or a chat page on Facebook be detrimental? It's just a TV show. It's just a movie. It's just a video game. It's just the Internet. Right?
Wrong.

The Neurology of Habits

Nothing is "just" anything when it comes to the constant, persistent exposure to media on a young brain. Neurologically, nearly everything we encounter has a potential shaping effect—chemically, physiologically and psychologically—as it works its magic or its mayhem on the developing brain. Nearly everything we encounter through our senses becomes a part of us for a brief time, and some of it actually becomes a permanent part of who we are and what we believe.

The things in which we engage the most of our time are the things that tend to most easily and readily hardwire our brains. Whether it's porn, or online gaming, or *World of Warcraft,* or www.movieguide.com, or www.worship.net, or www.faithink.com, the things in which we immerse ourselves again and again and repeatedly set our hearts and minds on do not simply *shape* our hearts and minds; they eventually *become* our hearts and minds. The healthy things we consume will eventually have a healthy effect on us, while the unhealthy things we consume will eventually consume us. Garbage in; garbage out. It's true for computer programming, and it's even truer for the human minds.

What we feed our children's bodies eventually gets used, and the worthless and empty stuff is flushed out. What we feed our children's brains, however, gets used but may never be flushed away. The messages that are fed repeatedly—no matter how worthless— become a permanent part of their lives.

That is true for the Bread of Life, and it is also true for sawdust and manure. But why?

Why Habits Are Hard to Break

Your brain tends to develop "grooved pathways" that favor those habits you feed and nurture the most. The earlier you get started in a habit, the easier that habit is to imprint, and the longer it will last. It's as simple and complex as that. Once a habit is formed, you will tend to lean toward that direction the rest of your life. French scientist Léon Dumond put it this way:

> Flowing water hollows out a channel for itself which grows broader and deeper; and when it later flows again, it follows the path traced by itself before. Just so, the impressions of outer objects fashion for themselves more and more appropriate paths in the nervous system, and these vital paths recur under similar external stimulation, even if they have been interrupted for some time.[31]

In other words, the more you expose yourself to something— whether good or bad—the more easily it becomes a part of you. If you fix your heart and mind on the heart and mind of Christ, the heart and mind of Christ will fix upon you and in you. If you fill your children's lives and schedules with the good things of God, they will lean toward the good things of God the rest of their lives. Here's the good stuff that God wants to fix in your child's life:

> The fruit of the Spirit is love, joy, peace, patience, kindness, generosity, faithfulness, gentleness, and self-control (Gal. 5:22-23).

Who wouldn't want these gifts at the forefront of their children's hearts, minds and imaginations? Who wouldn't want their
children drifting off to sleep with the peace and presence of these
good and godly gifts filling their dreams every night? But how can
we possibly hardwire the good things of God when day in and day
out we're sitting in a giant pile of sawdust and manure?

A Neurology of the Word

Please allow the amateur neurologist in me to get way too technical
for a moment. Nerve cells are the ultimate "use me or lose me"
mechanisms. New baby neurons—birthed from stem cells in the
short-term "scratch pad" (hippocampus)—punch out by the thousands every day and night, saying, "Put me to work!" Half of these
nerve cells don't last more than a few days. Those that receive instructions and act on them soon after birth will grow, thrive and
hardwire, but those that don't receive instructions and act on them
will wither, die and disappear.

Every time you experience, sense or think about something new,
a new little bundle of neurons is assigned the job of receiving, registering and doing something with that new information. Every new
stimuli, every new thought, every new sensation, every new picture,
and every new experience is registered and attached to a neural network that has a chance of becoming a part of you. However, for
these neurons to move from the "scratch pad" (hippocampus) to
the "hard drive" (neo cortex), they must quickly be repeated, re-
thought or re-experienced. If they get a second shot at rethinking,
reacting, or re-firing, they have a chance of strengthening, linking to
other neurons, and moving into long-term storage.

Okay, here's the technical part. According to Nicholas Carr:

> Whenever an experience is repeated, the synaptic links be-
> tween the neurons grow stronger and more plentiful. Every
> time you repeat an action, a thought, a new word, there are
> both physiological and anatomical changes. Each repetition
> releases a higher concentration of chemical neurotransmit-

ters to make the bond stronger. Each repetition also causes the growth of more new neurons, more connections (synapses) on the end of existing neurons, and more receptors for the chemicals in those neurons.[32]

Baby nerve cells that receive and retrieve sensory instructions and act on those instructions will strengthen if those instructions are repeated soon after the initial input. If repeated often enough, they will link to more neurons, forming whole networks devoted to the new thinking, skill or movement. With practice, these rapid-fire connections strengthen, get more efficient in firing, and grow an even thicker and more connected network.

With enough practice, the memory, thought or action etched on the hard drive will become a part of who we are, what we think and what we believe. The more often these neurons fire, the quicker they will hardwire and the deeper the habit will embed. Carr continues:

> Once a habit is formed—whether good or bad—the brain strains to keep that habit in place. As particular circuits in our brain strengthen through the repetition of a physical or mental activity, they begin to transform that activity into a habit. The paradox of neuroplasticity (the brain's ability to change, grow and rewire) is that, for all the mental flexibility it grants us, it can end up locking us into rigid behaviors. The chemically triggered synapses that link our neurons program us, in effect, to want to keep exercising the circuits they've groomed. Once we've wired new circuitry into our brain, we long to keep it activated. That's the way the brain fine-tunes its operations.[33]

That's the way our brains form both good and bad habits. That's the way they memorize a song, a phone number, a computer access code, a golf swing, or the talent to hotwire an engine and get us convicted of grand theft auto. That's how good and great habits of reading and singing and empathy and compassion and joy become part and parcel of who a child will be. That's also how God's

Word, will and wisdom can be hardwired into a young brain. It's the process and method by which bad habits started early in life become so hard to break. It's just easier for a brain to keep doing what it has been trained to do.

Proverbs 22:6 states, "Train children in the right way, and when old, they will not stray." Do you recognize the wisdom of this proverb? It isn't just good parenting advice—it's brilliant neurology. God must have read some of those brain books.

Part II: Fill 'er Up (with the Good Stuff)

An Encouraging Secret

Let me tell you an encouraging secret: the brain can just as easily learn a healthy habit as a bad one. If you introduce your children to the practice of sharing highs and lows, reading God's Word, and then applying that Word to their highs and lows, you will be giving them a tool that will bless their lives. You will be teaching them to see the positive, to be honest about the negative, and to concentrate together on healthy solutions and resolutions. As Paul wrote in Philippians 4:8-9:

> Finally, beloved, whatever is true, whatever is honorable, whatever is just, whatever is pure, whatever is pleasing, whatever is commendable, if there is any excellence and if there is anything worthy of praise, think about these things. Keep on doing the things that you have learned and received and heard and seen in me, and the God of peace will be with you.

Focus on these qualities, and they will come to live in your and your children's hearts and minds. But let your mind be filled with whatever comes across the airwaves or the screen, and the crass, false, cynical, impure, dishonorable will become a part of you. Whatever captures the most of your time and attention will eventually become part of you . . . then much of you . . . then most of you. Just as the good can become you, the bad can become you as well.

Garbage in; garbage out. Good stuff in; good stuff out.

Giving the Best

As a Christian parent, you know you cannot give the best to your children unless you introduce them to Jesus. The Holy Spirit makes this introduction most effectively through your witness, your loving and consistent care, and your help in making it easy and fun for them to ingest and digest the Word of God.

You can't (and won't) always be there physically for your children. There may come a day when they can't, don't or won't want to listen to you for a while. There may come a day when they see your flaws and think you're an idiot. (For many parents, that day is called adolescence—and it can be a pretty long day!) Yet whether that day comes or not, your children need to see you pointing away from yourself and toward their perfect heavenly Father—the God who is ever faithful, ever loving and ever wise. They may not listen to your words, but they will always listen to your example. May you be a living Bible this day!

A Theology of the Word

So, what does God's Word do? At the beginning of my doctoral work, I traveled to 100 cities in the United States and Australia and asked parents, pastors and youth workers to share what they believe God's Word does in our lives. Here are some of their most common answers:

- The Word enlightens us, teaches us and provides guidance to us (it "forms" us as it "informs" us).
- The Word convicts us of our sin and admonishes us.
- The Word strengthens and empowers us.
- The Word blesses us and brings us joy.
- The Word heals us and brings us wisdom.

- The Word gives us eternal answers.
- The Word equips us and motivates us.
- The Word engenders grace and love in our lives.
- The Word builds us up in faith and hope.
- The Word reveals God's truth to us and makes God become real.
- The Word helps us experience God.
- The Word shows that God is bigger than us.
- The Word gives us insight into the mind and will of God.
- The Word deepens our roots.
- The Word causes us to become part of God's story.
- The Word helps us feel connected with God over time.
- The Word helps us see God at work in and through us.
- The Word gives us individuals with whom we can identify.
- The Word brings release; we get a new lease on life.
- The Word gives us peace.
- The Word shows us how to receive forgiveness.
- The Word helps us see God at work in our lives.
- The Word causes us to become attached to God's people.
- The Word makes us more aware of answers to problems.
- The Word sets up the maxim that when we get into God's Word, God's Word gets into us.

Whew! What a list! Why wouldn't you want to give your children these good, godly, amazing gifts every night of their young lives? Allow me to wax poetic a moment:

God's Word is power
God's Word is sound
God's Word's a shower
On parched, dry ground
God's Word's a candle
God's Word is light
A beacon piercing
The darkest night
The darkest night

Dr. Rich Melheim

God's Word is presence
God's Word is peace
God's Word is healing
Hope, faith, release
This living whisper
This loving Lord
God's Word's a thunder
A mighty sword
A mighty sword

A sword that heals
An oak that sways
A song that steals
All breath away
God's Word's an anchor
God's Word's a sail
To hold and launch you
It cannot fail
It will not fail

I like to tell people where to go. You should, too. Go to the Word of God.

The Altar that Alters

God's Word is an altar that alters us. It is a light that lights and enlightens us. It is a seed that seizes, sees and seeds us. Placed on the home altar, it will alter our homes, our hearts, our identities, our families and the future. I once texted my doctoral mentor, Leonard Sweet, a thought: "The home altar will alter the home." Moments later, he responded, "And the altar ego will alter the id!" (In other words, bringing your ego to God's altar every night will shape and change your identity!)

God's Word is a story that stories, re-stories and restores us. It is a tale as big as all time, yet God's story is our story as well. It is as communal and timeless as a melody that spans millennia, yet as personal and intimate as our own secret dreams, hopes and prayers. God's Word is a sword that slices both ways—a scalpel that cuts even as it heals. When we attach ourselves to God's Word, it attaches to us and won't let us go until it blesses us. It does not change, but it will always change us. It cannot change, but it will change us.

Historically Illiterate Children

With 3,000,000,000 copies in print and an estimated 6,000,000,000 copies sold since its first printing, the Bible is the bestselling book of all time. It has sold 2 billion more copies than the next 100 books combined. Its stories, language and teachings form the foundation of everything from the *Magna Carta* to the *Declaration of Independence* to the core themes of most human rights charters and the best-selling books and films ever produced. Yet most people today don't know much at all about the Bible. Most can't tell Abraham from Moses or Sarah from Ruth. Many think Joan of Arc was Noah's wife.

In an article titled "Why Public Schools Should Teach the Bible" in the *Wall Street Journal*, actress Roma Downey and producer Mark Burnett argued that "Westerners cannot be considered literate without a basic knowledge of this foundational text." They went on to state:

> Without the Bible, Shakespeare would read differently— there are more than 1,200 references to Scripture in his works. Without the Bible, there would be no Sistine Chapel and none of the biblically inspired masterpieces that hang in countless museums worldwide. In movies, without biblical allegories, there would be no *Les Misérables*, no *Star Wars*, no *Matrix*, no *Lord of the Rings* trilogy, no *Narnia* and no *Ben-Hur*. There would be no Alcoholics Anonymous, Salvation Army or Harvard University—all of which found their roots in Scripture. And really, what would Bono sing about if there were no Bible?
>
> Can you imagine students not reading the Constitution in a U.S. government class? School administrators not shar-

ing the periodic table of the elements with their science classes? A driver's ed course that expected young men and women to pass written and road tests without having access to a booklet enumerating the rules of the road? It would be the same thing, we believe, to deny America's sons and daughters the benefits of an education that includes a study of the Bible.[34]

To raise a child without a thorough knowledge of the core stories that shaped Western civilization is to raise a culturally and historically illiterate child. I suggest we change that one night at a time. One story at a time.

A Gift Like No Other

The Bible is more than a history or mystery book. It's more than a religious instruction manual or "Basic Instructions Before Leaving Earth" (B.I.B.L.E.). My momma taught me that the Bible is essentially a love letter.

The Bible is God's love letter to the world, because it reveals God's loving heart. In the pages of the Bible, God names our hearts and claims our hearts. It is a story of God's loving heart seeking our broken hearts. Immersing our hearts and minds in God's Word gives us experience with and access to the wisdom, will and wonder of the Almighty God of the universe—the God who created us and loved us enough to die for us.

God's written Word is priceless—a gift like no other gift you can give your children—precisely because through it the Holy Spirit leads people to find God's Living Word, Jesus Christ. And through Jesus, we find eternal life.

The Living Word, Jesus Christ, cannot be contained in time and space, let alone in the letters and words on a page. Yet through the Bible, this Living Word comes alive again as the Holy Spirit calls, gathers and enlightens God's people. Jesus is the very heart of God. Read the Bible searching for Jesus from cover to cover, and you will find more than you could ever expect.

Do you want to know the heart of God? Take a look at Jesus. Do you want to know the will of God? Take a look at Jesus. Do you want to know the mind, wisdom, wonder and power of God? You know what to do. Here is a verse for each night of the week on the beauty, depth and wonder of the Word:

Sunday:

God's Word feeds: "One does not live by bread alone, but by every word that comes from the mouth of God" (Matt. 4:4).

Monday:

God's Word seeds: "Now the parable is this: The seed is the word of God" (Luke 8:11).

Tuesday:

God's Word saves: "For I am not ashamed of the gospel; it is the power of God for salvation to everyone who has faith, to the Jew first and also to the Greek" (Rom. 1:16).

Wednesday:

God's Word equips: "All scripture is inspired by God and is useful for teaching, for reproof, for correction, and for training in righteousness, so that everyone who belongs to God may be proficient, equipped for every good work" (2 Tim. 3:16-17).

Thursday:

God's Word cuts deep: "Indeed, the word of God is living and active, sharper than any two-edged sword, piercing until it divides soul from spirit, joints from marrow; it is able to judge the thoughts and intentions of the heart" (Heb. 4:12).

Friday:

God's Word heals: "He sent out his word and healed them, and delivered them from destruction" (Ps. 107:20).

Saturday:

God's Word endures: "The grass withers, the flower fades; but the word of our God will stand forever" (Isa. 40:8).

Speaking of endurance, I'd like to tell you about God's Word and my mother's last gift.

Part III: Saying Goodbye to Mom

The Greatest Gift

On the night my mother died, I lay in bed and wept—not so much in grief, but in thanks for all the marvelous gifts she had given to enrich and sustain my life. Mom planted many beautiful seeds in me—seeds for which I am and will be eternally grateful. But of all the gifts she gave and all the seeds she planted, I believe her love for reading in general, and for reading God's Word in specific, were by far the best.

We had celebrated Kathryn Marie's seventy-sixth birthday in the hospital with cupcakes the day after she broke her hip. We blessed her and prayed with her when she decided to have the surgery, knowing her frail body might not survive, but knowing that spending the rest of her life in bed wasn't what she wanted either.

We laughed when, prior to the operation, the doctor asked, "Do you want us to attempt any extraordinary measures if something should happen during surgery and your heart should stop?" When Mom asked what the doctor meant, he said, "Do you want us to pound on your chest?" She thought for a moment, scratched her chin and replied, "Oh, maybe just a little. But don't go to any trouble."

Mom always had such a great sense of perspective. And humor. And direction. And faith. She knew where she was going. If she lived, she lived to the Lord, and if she died, she died to the Lord. As far as she was concerned, whether she lived or whether she died, she would be just fine.

We kissed, cried and prayed when Mom went into surgery. We cried and prayed again when she came out of the operating room wearing a full-faced oxygen mask but didn't wake up. We waited and prayed and hoped against hope as her kidneys began to shut down. We pleaded with her to open her eyes and say her goodbyes when her grandchildren came into the room. We held our breath when her eyes fluttered open one last time to see them, and we thought we sensed a faint smile on her parched lips.

Then, one week and a day from her sterile cupcaked birthday party, we said our goodbyes and stood at the bedside as they took her off life support. The teacher, wife, mother and friend spent her last hours on this side of eternity surrounded by family as they watched, waited and sang her favorite hymns from one end of the songbook to the other all day long and into the night.

Exhausted, we took Dad home to get some rest at 10:30 PM, leaving baby sister Karen at Mom's bedside to keep watch through the darkness. An hour later we received the call. Mom was gone.

As I lay half-sleeping, half-weeping in thanks for such a mom as this, two things came to mind. First, all her life, the teacher had taught me how to live. And now with her death, she had taught me how to die.

Mom's View of Daily Bread

My mother believed God's Word had power to accomplish great things. She made sure her children were in the pew with her and ready for Sunday School every Sunday. But worship and Sunday School weren't the end of our Christian education in the Melheim house. They were the start of a weeklong encounter with the Word.

Along with nightly prayers at the top of the stairs, Mom made sure the Word was central to our daily lives. To remind herself to do this, she kept a little brown plastic Daily Bread box in the middle of the kitchen table. There was bread, and then there was Daily Bread. Mom made sure we knew the value and always had the best of both.

Much to our later adolescent impatience and dismay, we literally couldn't get up from the table in our house until we shared a Scripture verse together from that little Daily Bread box, and then closed our mealtime with the prayer, "O give thanks unto the Lord; for he is good; for his mercy endureth for ever" (1 Chron. 16:34, *KJV*).

Digesting Scripture along with our meal and praying in thanksgiving before we dashed off was smart neurology. Studies show that babies, the brain-damaged and your average teenager all learn in the same way. Messages must come to the brain loud, clear, repeated, reinforced and interconnected. With this simple ritual, Mom was able to instill in us something all adolescents (and adults acting like adolescents) could really use these days: an attitude of constant gratitude. If we balked, the Wisconsin farm girl-turned-teacher would simply smile, wink and whisper, "Only the pigs at the trough don't stop to say thank you!"

Mom's faith didn't stop at the Bible. It started there and reached out to the hurting of the world. In my growing years, there wasn't a Thanksgiving, Christmas or Easter that our dining table wasn't filled with a dozen widows, widowers, college students, loners and strays. My sisters and I grew up spending every holiday setting up extra chairs, unfolding extra card tables, and waiting on these old wrinkled saints and loners. The dear Norwegian pietist could not even think of leaving the lonely alone on what could be the most depressing days of the year. We tried to be a family for them. A spiritual home. A little piece of their identity.

Unspoken Sermons

Mom modeled her love for the Word through her actions, but also through a worn, marked, open Bible sitting in her sunroom. For 38 years as the pastor's wife, she led women's Bible studies in our parlor, in our basement and sometimes in our garage. Her favorite subject included dressing up and acting out the lives of women from the Bible—for which she had written 22 studies and skits. Her second favorite teaching topic was the Revelation of John.

When the Hal Lindsey crowd was predicting the eminent end of the world, Mom's teaching was simple: "Look, Jesus said He didn't even know exactly when the end was coming, so if God has let you in on it, I want to meet you. You must be smarter than Jesus!" And, "Whether the end of the world will come in 10 minutes or 10,000 years, I don't know. The fact is, the end of *your* world is coming in your lifetime. You could get hit by a bread truck tomorrow. You need to get right with Jesus now!"

Mom's summary of the Revelation was simple: "Write these two words and an exclamation point under the book title in your Bible. These words are all you need to remember when your world is falling apart—Jesus wins!"

The Whispered Song

After I received the phone call about my mother's death, I lay in bed, half asleep, half awake in prayer, thinking about her grace, face and faith. As I drifted in and out, the Holy Spirit whispered Scripture to my ear:

> If we live, we live to the Lord and if we die, we die to the Lord. So then, whether we live or whether we die, we are the Lord's (Rom. 14:8).

Kathryn Marie believed this with all her heart. I fell asleep. About an hour later, I stirred again and woke to another whisper:

> Listen, I will tell you a mystery! We will not all die, but we will all be changed, in a moment, in the twinkling of an eye, at the last trumpet. For the trumpet will sound, and the dead will be raised imperishable (1 Cor. 15:51-52).

This second dream verse didn't come as words alone. It came with a melody. I rose and scratched the tune out on a notepad by the bed, and then drifted off again. A week after my mother's funeral, I gave it to Todd Ernster, a brilliant musical friend and founder of the Minnesota Music Hall of Fame band The Killer Hayseeds. Todd invited his lead singer, Ross Florand, into his studio, and the two spent a night turning it into a quiet country ballad. Ross was raised a Christian, but he didn't consider himself much of one at the time. But something about that verse hit him just right that night, and a silent seed was sown.

Listen to the Scripture song for **1 Corinthians 15:51-52** at www.faith5.org/extras.

Months later, Ross's own mother died. When the pastor visited the family before the funeral, he asked if there were any special Bible passages they would like to have read. No one had a Scripture in mind, so the pastor gave some options, including Romans 14:8 and 1 Corinthians 15:51-52. When Ross heard the words, "If we live, we live to the Lord," he recognized the verse and perked up. "Yeah, I know that one," he said. "I like that. Read that one."

As the pastor preached a powerful sermon about faith, hope and trusting in the love of God, the silent seeds grew. There, at his mother's funeral, Ross met the Living Word—Jesus—in the Living Word. After the funeral, he told his family and friends he would return to the Jesus who had never left him in the first place.

The Killer Hayseeds were stunned when, shortly after that, Ross's own heart stopped suddenly and unexpectedly. "It's ironic for someone with that big of a heart to have heart disease," our friend Todd wrote in Ross's obituary.[35]

Planting Seeds

In Isaiah 55:10-11, the prophet Isaiah writes:

> For as the rain and the snow come down from heaven, and do not return there until they have watered the earth, making it bring forth and sprout, giving seed to the sower and bread to the eater, so shall my word be that goes out from my mouth; it shall not return to me empty, but it shall accomplish that which I purpose, and succeed in the thing for which I sent it.

My mother's life planted God's Word in my heart while I was growing up, and my mother's death planted God's Word in my head. On the night she died, the Holy Spirit whispered the Word in a song. Later, the song planted itself in another son's head, and it returned at another mother's funeral. Then the Word took root in a

Listen to the Scripture song for Isaiah 55:10-11 at www.faith5.org/extras.

Country Western singer's heart and brought him back to Jesus just before he died.

That song was a gift, but it wasn't my mother's last gift. There would be one more.

The Morning After

The morning after Mom died, I awoke and stepped out into the sunroom porch where she always did her morning devotions. I sat down in her sacred sunroom space, a cup of coffee steaming nearby and the sunlight streaming through her window, and glanced down at her table. There, waiting for me in the center of a pile of a dozen spiral-bound notebooks, was our little brown Daily Bread box. A handwritten note scrawled on a yellow Post-It note read:

> Richy Dear, in these binders you will find my notes on 22 women of the Bible. These pages include Bible studies, activities and skits I composed and taught over the last 50 years at church. I wonder if you'd finish them up for me and help me spread the Word? Maybe call it "Women of the Word" or "WOW!" Catchy title, don'cha think?

For the next 22 days, I typed up one of mom's studies each day and turned it into a Bible Study course called *WOW* (*Women of the Word*). I had to do it. It was both my therapy and my way of saying one last thank you.[36]

May my brilliant teacher mom continue to teach from her grave.

Home Huddle: How to Start

After a little exercise and sharing highs and lows, open your Bibles and immerse yourselves in a key Scripture story for the night. Verses

---

Access the 22 **WOW (Women of the Word) lessons** by Kathryn Marie Melheim
at www.faith5.org/extras.

---

can be chosen in numerous ways, depending on your preference, including the following.

One Verse Each Night

Some people like to read through the Bible from one end to the other by reading one verse each day. My friend Pastor Bob Mooney in Yorba Linda, California, calls this a "spiritual vitamin." ("You give your children a One-a-Day in the morning. Why not give them One-a-Night? You give them a Flintstone in the morning. Why not give them something from the Real Bedrock tonight?")

If you wish to tackle a single verse each night, check your local Christian bookstore for calendars, journals and daily reading schedules. Google "verse of the day" and you'll see more than 50 million results (that's a few too many sites to research). One of my favorite resources for a thorough cover-to-cover Bible reading is the Ezra Project's "Chronological Bible Reading Journal" found at http://www.ezraproject.net/products.html.

One Story Each Week

If you have younger children, there is a great neurological argument for sticking to the same Bible verse or story all week until they develop mastery of it. Bouncing from theme to theme before your kids fully understand the story is like bounding from wave to wave without a chance to go deep. Stay with the story all week, apply your new highs and lows each night, and you and your children will grow both in biblical literacy and in a deeper understanding of the story.

If you wish to cover one story each week, I've provided a full year of fun and interactive Bible readings in appendix A to get you started. This schedule will expose your family to 30 key stories in the Old Testament (Creation to Job) and 22 from the life and teachings of Jesus (from His birth to His resurrection and ascension). Full-color cartoon home journals for each of these themes are available at http://www.faithink.com/Inkubators/biblesong_living.asp.

Connecting Church to Home

The best way to gain a deeper understanding of each Bible story (I call it a "frame of reverence") is to convince your pastor to preach on the same themes that you are learning in your Christian education program.

Ask your church to launch the story for the week in both settings and to print a key central Scripture from that story in a bulletin or handout that you can use every night during FAITH5 time. Highlight or underline that verse in your Bibles. Then sing it, sign it in American Sign Language, and create art and skits with it on Sunday. Celebrate it in multiple ways at church, and then bring the story and key verse home to use it for your FAITH5 theme all week long.

There is an entire FAITH5 worship-to-home "Bible Song" curriculum available for churches, homeschools and family.

Download free sample lessons with links to fun cartoon stories, Scripture songs, American Sign Language, games and cartoon color pages at http://www.faithink.com/Inkubators/bssintro1.asp.

Dream Team Reflections

Your word is a lamp to my feet and a light to my path.
PSALM 119:105

Gather with your family, friends or a small group of people you trust and respect to share the following.

Theme Verse
Read and highlight today's theme verse in your Bible, and then hop online to the link below to learn this verse in song and American Sign Language.

Reflection 1
What do you treasure? If your house happened to be on fire and you only had time to save a few things, what (or who) would you grab first, second and third?

To watch videos on this theme, learn **Psalm 119:105** in song and American Sign Language, and download free weekly devotional resources, go to www.faith5.org/read.

Reflection 2

If someone you really wanted to meet asked you "what's your story," how would you answer? If they pressed further and said, "I'm intrigued; tell me, who and what matters to you, and why," how would you respond?

Reflection 3

What happens to a person when he or she . . .

- Reads and reflects on God's Word every day?
- Makes his or her home a "house of the Lord" every night?
- Reflects on God's Word just prior to going to sleep every night?

This Week's Challenge

Commit to trying the first two steps of FAITH5 every night before bedtime this week. Whoever is going to bed first calls "huddle up!" or "FAITH5!" or "highs and lows—five minutes!" and names the room for sharing. Use the free *Read Home Huddle Journal* download at www.faith5.org/read/weekly to record your highs and look up the Scriptures in your Bible. Read the passage and highlight it together. If you are living alone, commit to calling a friend or family member every night this week to ask them to share their highs and lows. Then read the Scripture together. In addition, you may want to consider:

- Watching me discuss the power of reading God's Word at www.faith5.org/read/rich
- Watching the Gillunds tell their FAITH5 family story at www.faith5.org/read/story
- Learning this week's Bible verse, Psalm 119:105, in song and American Sign Language with Christy Smith at www.faith5.org/read/song

You can also download weekly resources, nightly Bible verses, videos, games and other free resources at www.faith5.org/read/weekly.

Talk

Keep these words that I am commanding you today in your heart.
Recite them to your children and talk about them when you are at home
and when you are away, when you lie down and when you rise.
DEUTERONOMY 6:6-7

The third step of FAITH5 is to talk about how a key Bible text or story might relate to your highs and lows of the day.

On some days it will be obvious how God's story intersects with your own, while on other days it may not seem like it applies at all. Be creative. Look for links and connections. Ask, "What is God trying to say to my life?" or "What does this verse mean to me today?" You can choose your verses from anywhere—your church's Sunday preaching/teaching texts, from a favorite devotional book, from the free handouts at www.faith5.org, from appendix A of this book, or even from a *FAITH5 Home Huddle Journal*.[1]

A FAITH5 Family Story

Michael Diamond grew up with a physically abusive father.[2] As a child he prayed that God would make the beatings stop, but his prayers were unanswered. He gave up on God until he met Shannon.

To learn **Deuteronomy 6:6-7** in song and American Sign Language,
go to www.faith5.org/talk/song.

The two fell in love, but Shannon told him she couldn't marry him unless he came back to God. So he started attending church, and later they were married. They tried to start a family but experienced fertility issues. It was then that Michael's prayer life began to deepen. "I promised God that if we were blessed with a child, I'd make a commitment to raise the child the best way I could." Soon after, they were blessed with two boys: Thomas and Patrick.

When little Patrick was diagnosed with a rare and deadly cancer, Michael, who had served on nuclear submarines in the Navy, launched into a frantic research project. He attended genetic research conferences and talked with the top minds in the world, searching for a cure. "Finally, I just woke up one day and a sense of peace came over me," Michael says. "I said, 'God, there is nothing I can do about this.' And the sense of peace I had was almost like a drug." Michael turned the whole situation over to God, and with prayer, the support of his church, the brilliant people at St. Jude Children's Hospital and a thousand little miracles, little Patrick is still alive today.

Michael is bound and determined to give his boys everything he didn't have growing up. That's where FAITH5 has blessed them. Six weeks into testing it at their bedtime routine, both Michael and Shannon are amazed at the depth of talking the boys are doing. "As a parent, there are no words to describe the euphoria you feel when your five-year-old child is able to articulate his feelings and faith," says Michael. "What I'm hoping to get from this is to save my kids from having to go through the trials and tribulations, heartache and misery I went through to finally have my eyes opened. If I can save them from that misery and pain, I feel that as a parent I've done the best job I could do."

Every night in the Diamond home, the wind-down starts with a pillow fight. "There was a night about a week or so ago when we were so frustrated and so tired," says Shannon. "Everybody was cranky, so I got out the pillows.

Our pillow fight broke that tension and melted away the frustration. We were able to get down to our FAITH5 and praising and go to bed feeling much better than we did 10 minutes before."

Shannon sees FAITH5 as a tool that can help her family weather any crisis that might arise down the road. "If someone tells you, 'Hey, your kid's got cancer,' you don't have the choice of going back to bed, pulling the covers up and pretending they didn't tell you," she says. "You have to fight. One of the fears with a cancer as vicious as Patrick's is that it's likely to return. Now that we have FAITH5 and Skype, even if we have to again be separated across two states for treatment, I know that every night we can get on our computers and still do this. We can still talk. It'll be something that will help us all stay connected."

Part I: Technology or "Talk-Knowledgy"

The Psychology of Talk

Think for a moment about talking as both a talent and a technology. Every new technology we employ literally changes our brains. *New York Times* writer Nicholas Carr explains, "For human beings, language is the primary vessel of conscious thought. The technologies that restructure language tend to exert the strongest influence over our intellectual lives."[3]

Talking is a technology that can change our brains and our lives. Like muscles, whatever we exercise the most in the brain grows. When stories and oral tradition were the main delivery systems of people's culture and identity, their brains grew a greater capacity in the areas of linguistics, phonics, memory, imagination and meaning. When print technology showed up and was embraced, people's brains developed more capacity in connecting the eyes to sound and meaning. When radio showed up, people's ears were again more attached to the imagination centers of the brain. When TV appeared, things changed yet again. TV feeds us our images and sounds.

Today we don't have to imagine as much, so the imagination areas of our brains have withered even as the visual and sound areas have grown. We live on the edge of a new set of Internet technologies, which Carr describes as "skimming over the surface of life on a speed jet, bouncing from wave to wave at breathtaking speeds. It's a rush, and the areas of our brain that adjust quickly are growing in speed and efficiency. What we're losing is our capacity to go deep . . . to go under the wave, to slow down and make meaning of it all."[4]

Tourist to Officer: How do you get to Carnegie Hall?
Officer: Practice, practice, practice.

Going Deep

Some believe that as a culture, we are losing our ability to go deep. To think deep thoughts. To imagine deep meaning.

If you've ever snorkeled or taken a scuba dive, you have learned that the ocean is much deeper and richer than it appears to those who only skim the surface. You have experienced the slow, quiet depths of the sea and now have a richer awareness and appreciation of its wonder than those who merely bounce from wave to wave. You have seen a different kind of light, a different kind of life, a different kind of power and a deeper, richer meaning of the sea.

Surface speeders may have a hint that there is something else down there, but until they consciously decide to turn the key and ditch the jet for an immersion in the silence beneath the waves, they won't know what they are missing. In the same way, this entire generation of "teched up" children will never know how to go deep if they don't ever experience going deep.

The word "text" used to be a noun. It once was a word on a page—something to be read, studied, discussed, pondered and applied to our lives. Today, "text" is a verb—an action word. In a world where more people are opting to text than to talk, and where twitters and tweets and abbreviations are condensing conversations to 140 characters or less, the art of deep conversations, deep listening and deep thought is rapidly disappearing.

How do you grow deep-thinking, deep-listening and deep-caring kids? How do you enrich your nightly ritual in a way that turns your home into a place of true depth, care and understanding? How do you go deep? The answer is simple: *you go deep*. Let me explain.

You Got Your Chocolate on My Peanut Butter

Back in the 1980s, Reese's came out of the marketing clutter with a commercial showing the collision of two hipsters on a city street. They smashed their chocolate and peanut butter together and proclaimed, "Two great tastes that taste great together!" When two things that normally don't go together collide, a whole new world of possibilities arises. Some say such collisions are the birthplace of true creativity and innovation.

Theologian Karl Barth suggested that preachers should enter the pulpit with "the Bible in one hand and the newspaper in the other." He wanted them to get relevant by carefully, creatively and consistently applying the text to the context. He wanted them to get real, get practical, speak to real issues or get out of the pulpit.

In a world where virtually no faith talk is happening in the home, a family that committed to following through on this enriching faith practice would grow children who looked for the deep things of God to apply to their lives seven days a week. Connecting God's text to our context (highs and lows) is doing theology! It's also modeling Deuteronomy 6 in a real, simple, practical way and building godly faith practices into the core of the family.

What would happen in your home if you entered every night with the Bible in one hand and your child's life in the other? Seeking

God's wisdom and the counsel of those who know and love you the most every night is a *great* way to raise a spiritually and emotionally deep kid! See if you can find connections between the following highs and lows and the accompanying Scriptures:

- *Today's high:* "I got an *A* on my math test."
- *Today's low:* "A bully was mean to me at school."
- *Today's Scripture:* "Be strong and courageous; do not be frightened or dismayed, for the Lord your God is with you wherever you go" (Josh. 1:9).

- *Today's high:* "I saw a beautiful rainbow."
- *Today's low:* "I found out my best friend is moving away."
- *Today's Scripture:* "I am with you always, to the end of the age" (Matt. 28:20).

- *Today's high:* "I got to play with my friends."
- *Today's low:* "Some kids were mean to the new kid at school, and I didn't dare say anything."
- *Today's Scripture:* "Your kingdom come. Your will be done, on earth as it is in heaven" (Matt. 6:10).

- *Today's high:* "I can't think of one, except that Jesus loves me."
- *Today's low:* "I missed a goal and we lost the soccer match."
- *Today's Scripture:* "Why are you cast down, O my soul, and why are you disquieted within me? Hope in God; for I shall again praise him, my help and my God" (Ps. 42:5).

Some days it is easy to find the connections, while other days it's a stretch. But every day it can be fun to try. Like combining peanut butter with chocolate and coming up with something new and original (a Reese's peanut butter cup), mixing highs and lows with Scripture can lead to creative and innovative thinking.

The act of recalling and remembering the highs and lows of the day, and then turning and returning to God's Word, will create and reinforce memories and grooved pathways in the brain that will follow your children on through life. So set aside the time and the place to talk, and you will get what you are seeking. You will grow what you plant and nurture. You will see what you seed. You will become what you practice.

Guaranteed!

Include me out.
YOGI BERRA

Include Me Out

One night when our son, Joseph Martin, was about eight, he decided to test us during FAITH5 time. To see who was actually in charge of our family communication, he folded his little eight-year-old arms and announced to the family, "My high is my high and my low is my low. Next!"

Arlyce and I looked at each other for a moment, more amused than alarmed. We knew that handing over the decision about whether we would communicate as a family to a child who hadn't even yet hit hormones was ludicrous. It's great to empower your children, but transferring that particular power to a child who wouldn't have a fully developed prefrontal cortex (judgment center) for another 18 years would have been, well, really bad judgment. Let me say it another way: stupid.

We also knew that if we let our son stop talking at eight, we would be in real trouble by the time he turned 16. Recognizing this statement as a test of our parenting resolve, I calmly answered, "Look, if you don't have five minutes for your family tonight, you certainly don't have five minutes for Nintendo and Xbox and television and the Internet. If you don't have five minutes for your family, we will not have any five cents for your allowance. If you don't have five minutes . . ."

At that point, Joseph's sister, Kathryn Elizabeth, said something absolutely brilliant. She looked at him in all seriousness and said,

"Joseph! Open up! Share your pain! Girls think it's sexy!" Joseph didn't exactly know what "sexy" meant, but it sounded pretty good.

We didn't let him bow out of our family talk time at eight. There was too much at stake.

. . . .

King of Id: Remember the Golden Rule!
Sir Rodney: What's the Golden Rule?
King of Id: He who has the gold makes the rules!

. . . .

Who's Calling the Shots?

In the same way, a wise adult doesn't let the child run the family. Period. An intelligent adult doesn't turn the decisions about whether a child will get a tetanus shot over to the kid. ("I don't want to force little Mervin into this, or it might turn him off to shots the rest of his life.") There are certain things you know they need and, as an adult, you provide them whether they want them or not.

A loving adult doesn't let a toddler near a hot stove with boiling caramel bubbling on the burner. Sometimes "love" is best spelled "N-O." A caring adult doesn't take the training wheels off a bicycle until he or she knows the child is ready. A responsible adult does not let the teen decide whether or not to get up in the morning and go to school. That's a given. A thoughtful adult who knows the dangers of adolescence today does not let the child decide whether or not to check in, participate in the family, or keep the communication lines open.

By the way, as far as I am concerned, any faithful parent with half a brain doesn't let his or her children decide whether or not they will go to church with the family either. As a parent, you know what your kids need. You know the commandments of God to remember the Sabbath and honor your parents. You know the sawdust and manure their minds are consuming 24/7. You know the value of taking a break—a Sabbath—to dive deep into the ocean of worship. You know the promise you made to God when you first presented your child at church. You know your children won't have a fully developed prefrontal cortex (judgment center) in their brain until about the same year their car insurance rates go down (25 for women, 26 or 27 for men). You know what they need. So give it to them with no excuses.

Oh, yeah, you and your child should also know who's paying the bills. That's who gets to make the decisions in a real adult's house.

Never Too Late

Rex Miller is a friend of mine who is a sought-out speaker on trends and the future. We were keynoting a conference together a few years ago, and afterward he came up to me with a frown on his face. "Rich," he said, "I hear you about this nightly highs and lows and talking stuff, but I'm afraid it's too late for me. My son is 13 already. He's bigger than me. He's not going to go for any nightly conversations."

"Rex," I said, "who's in charge of your family?"

He looked at me for a painful moment, so I decided to take another, non-judgmental and practical tack. "Tell him you can hurt him financially."

"What?"

"Just tell him, 'If you won't talk to your dad every night—if you won't give me five minutes—I will not give you five cents when it comes time to pay for your car insurance!'"

Rex decided to take my advice. He announced that a nightly check-in would now be the default every night for as long as his son was under his roof. If I recall correctly, he also announced that this new decree wasn't up for debate, discussion or vote. (Remember the Golden Rule?) His son smirked, sighed and begrudgingly accepted the new world order. "Well, okay."

The next day, his son left for school, looking for highs and lows. That night he returned and said, "Okay, let's just do it!"

"Great," said Rex. "What was your high and low?"

"My low was easy. We had a pop quiz in math today, and I wasn't ready for it."

"And what was your high?" asked Rex.

The boy paused for a second, and then said with a sheepish grin, "The kid next to me was." An honest 13-year-old. What more could a parent want?

How do you build resilient children equipped to weather any storm? I believe it starts early with the stories you plant in their minds and the way you train them to see themselves in a story greater than their own.

The Neurology of Talk: Banks for the Memories (Throwing Highs, Lows and Scripture Together)

Contrary to popular opinion, learning, thoughts and memories are not held in banks waiting for a withdrawal. The human memory apparatus is more like a beehive, where the bees are constantly in motion, bringing in new sweet stuff, getting rid of old unused stuff, protecting the collective and collected valuable stuff, and feeding new, unformed baby ideas that haven't had a chance to hatch so that they can one day emerge and benefit the whole hive.

Memories are alive, active, rewiring and re-firing whenever we retrieve them—sometimes at will and sometimes at random. However, unlike a beehive (or a hard drive) that can only hold so much honey (or information), the human brain has a virtually unlimited memory supply. Storing new stuff doesn't bump the old stuff out or make it harder to reach. On the contrary, the more new stuff we put into our brains, the greater our capacity grows to learn even more.

Much like building up muscle by lifting weights, the act of talking, learning and thinking builds up an even greater capacity to talk, learn and think. As clinical psychologist Sheila Crowell explains, "Evidence suggests that as we build up our personal store of memories, our minds become sharper. The very act of remembering appears to modify the brain in a way that can make it easier to learn ideas and skills in the future."[5] Nicholas Carr agrees, stating, "With each expansion of our memory comes an enlargement of our intelligence."[6]

If you want to grow a child into an adult who can readily and easily find simple solutions to complex problems, give them a dose of sharing their highs and lows every night.

How the New Becomes the You

Unlike a bit, byte or gigabyte of information stored on a computer hard drive—which lives where it lives and doesn't bounce up against other bits, bytes and gigabytes—every new piece of information hardwired into your brain is ready and available to connect and enrich every other piece of information already stored there. Each and every nerve cell in your brain is connected to anywhere between 1,000 to 100,000 other nerves. That makes for 10,000 trillion possible unique connections. Multiply the number of connections times the number of possible combinations, and you get a 10 followed by a million zeros' worth of possible thoughts and creative combinations![7]

Here's a mind-boggler for you science buffs: the estimated number of possible connections in the human brain far exceeds the estimated number of particles in the universe.[8] Everything you put in can literally rub up against and connect to everything else you put in. Everything can literally inform, influence and transform everything else you know, do and want to be.

That's where good ideas come from. That's where genius is born. That's where what Stuart Kauffman describes as the "adjacent possible" allows for all the good you input to ruminate with all the other good and come up with something even greater:

> The strange and beautiful truth about the adjacent possible is that its boundaries grow as you explore them. Each new combination opens up the possibility of other new combinations. Think of it as a house that magically expands with each door you open. You begin in a room with four doors, each leading to a new room that you haven't visited yet. Once you open one of those doors and stroll into that room, three new doors appear, each leading to a

brand-new room that you couldn't have reached from your original starting point. Keep opening new doors and eventually you'll have built a palace.[9]

When you share your highs and talk out your lows, 10,000 trillion possible combinations of thought, insight and answers collide with 10,000 trillion other possible combinations from each brain in the room. Add to it the wisdom, depth and wonder of the Word of the God of the universe, and wow! What problem wouldn't you be able to solve?

Home as an Innovation Laboratory

Innovation expert Steven Johnson argues that the most creative ideas come from the collision of things that normally don't go together (remember the "you got your chocolate in my peanut butter" idea). Setting up a rich environment of diverse people, thoughts and challenges and allowing them to mix together in a non-judgmental atmosphere allows for new combinations and possibilities to arise. "Some environments squelch new ideas: some environments seem to breed them effortlessly,"[10] says Johnson. Just by putting together two things that normally don't belong—like your low today and the Bible verse—a new adjacent possibility arises.

Imagine raising a child who does creative problem solving in a living laboratory every night of his or her young life. Imagine a child who knows how to bring a problem out into the open, toss it out to a trusted cohort of friends, and work out solutions together. Your home would become a living laboratory of creativity. In that laboratory, you would raise up a wise little social scientist who knew whom to turn to with life's challenges, where to turn for creative problem solving with their loved ones, and how not only to meet a challenge but also to beat a challenge creatively.

Don't settle for a homeschool. Aspire to the status of home as an innovation laboratory.

Part II: What's at Stake Here?

Reuben and the Hittites

Years ago I met a fascinating teacher at a conference in Oregon. Reuben ben Yonathan grew up Jewish and converted to Christianity as a college student. Rueben asked me series of rhetorical questions: "Do you know any Hittites? Do you carpool with an Ammorite? Are you on the PTA with an Amalakite? No? Why? They disappeared. Why did they disappear? They forgot to tell their children their story, and if your children don't know their story, you don't lose your past. You lose your future."

Do your children know your faith story? Do they know the struggles, trials and plagues you and your people went through to get where you are today? Do they know how God got you through it all and how God is still leading you today? Do they know the dark nights of your soul when all you had to go on was a flickering candle of hope? Do they know of your wilderness wanderings when all you had was a wisp of a cloud to show the way? Do they know of your hungers and thirsts and the manna God provided to keep you going one day at a time?

If your children don't know your story—and how God held you when you couldn't hold yourself—they won't merely lose their past. They will lose their future.

 A person will worship something, have no doubt about that. . . . That which dominates our imaginations and our thoughts will determine our lives, and our character. Therefore, it behooves us to be careful what we worship, for what we are worshipping we are becoming.
RALPH WALDO EMERSON

The Promised Land

The Children of Israel had wandered in the wilderness for 40 years. When they were finally on the edge of the Promised Land, God gave Moses one last set of instructions to prepare the people. If you reread Deuteronomy 6:6-8, the theme verse for this step, it will become clear: God wanted Israel to saturate her children with the stories of faith and the Word of God.

Why did God want them to do this? Because the Promised Land wasn't empty. It was filled with people who practiced a strange, alluring and rather dangerous cult. There was child sacrifice in that land. There were temple prostitutes at the core of the religion. In official temples, atop the highest hills and under the greenest trees, they called the children to orgies every spring in order to cajole the gods Baal and Asherah into sending fertile rains, crops and flocks. The only way to protect their children in this dangerous land was to saturate their mornings, evenings, minds and hearts with the true things of God.

Now, you might object and say, "This is the twenty-first century. We don't have child sacrifice anymore. We don't have temple prostitutes enticing our children away from worshiping the one true God."

Guess again.

We sacrifice our children in temples to lesser gods all the time. We lay them on the altars of consumption, materialism, business and busyness. There are thousands of voices calling out to our children, "Come play with me, come lay with me!" On billboards, magazines, television and—scary to say—in our own homes on the new computers we just bought for Christmas, there are messages, messengers, massages and monsters approaching our children every night. It's not just sawdust. It's not just manure. It's poison.

If you don't talk with your children about your story when they lie down and when they rise, seeding it in their dreams and binding it on their memes, there will be many other voices and other stories just waiting in the wings to fill their hearts, minds and souls with a pantheon of compelling alternatives. The Bible tells us who we are and whose we are in the whole scheme of the universe. That message is both deep and wide.

So fill your children's lives and imaginations with God talk, God's story and your connection to God's story, and your children will grow up knowing they are precious children of the beautiful Savior, the king of creation. Leave your children alone to be filled and taught by television, peers and the "wise" of this world, and this is what they will hear:

God is dead. (Friedrich Nietzsche, philosopher and critic)

The more the universe seems to be determined, the more it seems pointless. (Steve Weinberg, Nobel Laureate physicist)

Let me summarize my views on what modern evolutionary biology tells us loud and clear. . . . There are no gods, no purposes, no goal-directed forces of any kind. There is no life after death. When I die, I am absolutely certain that I am going to be dead. That's the end for me. There is no ultimate foundation for ethics, no ultimate meaning to life, and no free will for humans, either. (William Provine, professor of biological sciences, Cornell University)

No goals? No future? No meaning? How could you live with such a philosophy? Why would you even try? Who could believe this, let alone bear it? Evidently, a lot of people. A study by the Prince Trust in England showed that 10 percent of 16- to 25-year-olds agree with the statement, "Life is meaningless and is not worth living."[11]

If there is no God, this world really is a miracle.
MELHEIMIAN MAXIM #9

The God-less Miracle

I have done a lot of reading and research in neuroscience during the last two decades, and I find most of it fascinating. Although

Christians, Jews and other people of faith work in the field, there are agnostics and atheists who believe we are nothing more than the sum of our parts—that there is no meaning, no purpose, no spirit, no soul and no "ghost in the machine."

I regularly chuckle when I read something written by agnostics and atheists and find words such as "design," "miraculous" and "the purpose of this mechanism" peppered throughout their works. They can't fully explain the mystery of transcendence people of faith experience, but they believe one day they will. And what about those stories of clinically dead people who came back relating details of what others said and did in their rooms when they were registering no brain wave activity? How do they deal with that issue? At best, they claim they were hallucinations registered by the brain when they were resuscitated—although I'm not sure how the brain can register anything if there are no brain waves doing the registering.

As far as I see it, if these folks have their way and neurology continues on its present trajectory—that of "pure mechanism"—eventually everything from love to loyalty to right and wrong will be one day thought to exist only in the gears of the machine. Everything from ethics, free will, morality, criminal behavior and legal culpability will be considered to be "caused" by the physical processes in our brains. Lady Gaga's "I Was Born this Way" will be a defense for every crime and misdemeanor. "How can I be blamed when I was born with these genes? My brain made me do it!"

If all we are is physical stuff, and if everything is determined by genes and outside forces, why should we care about others? About poverty? About hunger? About abuse? About anything other than ourselves, for that matter?

A God-less world is a meaningless world—and a colder, crueler and more heartless place as well. If Christians do not intentionally and intently fill their children's minds and hearts with the message of just how precious they are, those children will, by default, allow the world to tell another tale—that they are worthless and life is meaningless. That they are not precious and priceless. That they are nothing more than a fortunate and freakish accidental assembly of random atoms held together for a pointless, if not interesting, moment waiting to die. That they are merely sawdust and manure.

> How do you tell if a stick is straight? By putting it up next to a straight stick.
> G. K. CHESTERTON

Counterfeit Money

Here's a question for you: How do bank managers get bank tellers to recognize counterfeit money? The answer is that they saturate the tellers with authentic currency—the good stuff, the right stuff, the real stuff. Once the tellers know what the real currency looks like, the fake stuff is not as difficult to spot.

In the same way, how can we get our children to recognize the good from the bad? The healthy from the unhealthy? The genuine from the counterfeit? The True Bread from the loaf of sawdust and manure? Can there be spiritual maturation without biblical saturation?

I think not.

Contrary to this present the-universe-is-a-random-accident-and-your-meaningless-life-is-not-much-more worldview, the Bible gives us identity, worth and a role to play in the greatest love story of all time. The Bible shows us the God who created it all. The God who came again and again through the prophets, priests, shepherds and kings. The God who finally, at the fullness of time, came in flesh through the obedience of a peasant girl and the power of the Holy Spirit to walk among us.

This the God who came in love, grace and truth to rescue a loved but lost people. The God who abandoned it all for our sake, and then was abandoned by the very people He came to save. The God who went silently to the beatings, the cross and the grave for the lost He came to save. The God who went to hell for us so we wouldn't have to go ourselves. The God who went through hell to bring us to our home.

This is the God unfettered by time and space, who chose chains so that we could be set free. The God whose relentless love now waits for us on the other side of every hell, every challenge, every problem and every failure. The God whose fierce and tender love sighs for us with murmurs too deep for words to express. The God who cries for us, yearns for us, dies for us to come to our senses, and hops over fences to turn our wayward hearts to our one true home where we will always be welcomed whenever we wander. The God who waits for us on the other side of the grave, waiting to save us and give us eternity, life, peace, hope and more.

This is, truly, the greatest heart story, the greatest love story, the greatest war story, the greatest action adventure ever told. How can you not give this story to your children every night?

I don't know who God is. All I know is, He's a force more powerful than Mom and Dad put together. And you owe Him big time.

LISA SIMPSON

Back to Belles and Beaus

I noted in a previous chapter that little girls' brains are wired in the womb for more talk while little boys' brains are wired for more action. I also noted that whatever actions and skills people repeatedly practice will literally increase their neural network and, thus, their personal capacity to do the desired action more and more.

As a parent, you need to be aware of this fact and set practices in place to seed and foster your children's health. You cannot realistically expect your young son to express as many words and feelings during a conversation as compared to your daughter. However, you can make the decree known that everyone in the house is expected to share at least one high and one low—no matter how short.

As your children grow, you can also invite and encourage your children to contribute one insight into how they see the Bible verse for the night applying to those highs and lows. That's what the third step in FAITH5 is all about.

Let me run the risk of being politically incorrect and share an observation from my experience of working with children, youth and families. It appears to me that in our society, little girls and little boys often handle their pain, shame and pent-up frustrations in different ways. Little girls often tend to blame and punish themselves when they fail to deal with issues of shame, blame and pent-up pain in a healthy manner. (Anorexia, bulimia and cutting are the main problems seen in girls.) Even if a parent, teacher, coach, boyfriend or spouse abuses her, she may still have a tendency to blame herself or take partial responsibility for the abuse. "It was my fault. I shouldn't have . . ." They tuck the pain inside, and it eats away at them below the surface.

Little boys, on the other hand, are often more likely to blame and punish others when they don't know how to handle their pain—especially if they have had no experience or healthy outlets for dealing with it. Little girls tuck it in, internalize and punish themselves. Little boys push it out, externalize it and punish everyone else. Nearly every school shooter on record has been male.

In the United States, there are twice as many women in counseling for depression as men, and twice as many women attempt suicide. Yet twice as many men are locked up in mental institutions, and twice as many men commit suicide. The poet Henry David Thoreau described most men as "living lives of quiet desperation." If that is anywhere near true, it could be blamed on biology, but it also may be caused in part because boys are rarely exposed to the tools, practices, healthy male role models and safe sacred spaces where they can freely share their lows and gain perspective. Suffice it to say, if there is no outlet—and no experience with using the outlet—when the pressure builds, something is going to blow. Someone is going to pay.

The Latin root of the word "education" comes from *e+ducere*, meaning to lead out or draw out from within. As a parent, you need to draw out the highs and lows of both your belles and beaus so that they can deal with the issues in ways that will lead to their mental and emotional stability. Educating children on how to do this—and practicing the mechanisms each day—is a marvelous way to start.

What if we could teach our children healthy coping techniques from the cradle? What if we could teach them that someone has already paid for their pain, bled in their place, and went to hell so that they wouldn't have to do so? If they understood that His name is Jesus, and He is dying to set them free, they wouldn't have to go through life wanting to punish themselves or anyone else.

There is no reason to be a student of the future unless, of course, you plan to spend the bulk of the rest of your life there.

MELHEIMIAN MAXIUM #2

The Tech Talk of a Virtual Tomorrow

Even more dangerous and frightening than that literal tech world our children are virtually surrounded by today is the virtual tech world they will be literally surrounded by tomorrow. (I did the bulk of my doctorate for three years as an avatar on a 3D virtual island with Dr. Leonard Sweet and a cohort of 16 other avatars, and I know how much fun and how addictive this world can be.) In his book *Who Put My Life on Fast-Forward,* writer and futurist Phil Callaway offers a stark prophesy about the future of the virtual experience once it changes from a flat screen to true 3D: " 'Second Life' [a current cartoonish virtual world of online role-play games] is a transition space. When Google Earth gets online in full 3D, we can meet at the Eiffel Tower. All the screens will disappear. Everything will be holographic. The real question will be, 'Are you real?' "[12]

Callaway's comments should make every caring and protective parent—and everyone else who cares about the world of the future— think twice as hard and long. One day—possibly in our lifetimes but certainly in our children's lifetimes—we will all enter the holo-world. There is little question about it. The question is how, as technology improves and perfects, our children will know the real from the fake and the false from the true.

The holo-world will start as an amusement. Some folks will play in it only for entertainment—like a present-day video game. Some will choose to work there eight hours a day, and then come home and play there another eight hours. Some will put themselves on an IV nourishment drip and a urine bag to go on Virtual Vacations (VV) in Virtual Life (VL). Some will spend weeks there. Some won't return.

One day in our children's children's lifetime, those who can afford it will live mostly in VL, work mostly in VL, love mostly in VL. Human relationships will be seen as too messy, painful and uncomfortable. VL will become so advanced that most people won't know "real real" from "fake real." The fake real will fulfill their every wish.

VL will grant their every desire. Our species—or should I say those of our species who can afford it—will get everything they want, served up hot and spicy, 24-7. And they will *expect* to get everything they want, whenever they want it.

Objects that Object

How will we know the false from the real? Allow me to get way too technical and philosophical for a moment. In the VL world of the future, it may be that only the non-objects (the real) will object and tell us we can't have everything we want. Only they will push back. They will confront us and tell us we're being stupid when we need to hear it. They will cause us pain and refuse to give us our every desire.

The strange thing about that day for our species is that the *objects* (the virtual electronic beings) won't object and the *subjects* (as in real entities) will object when we treat them like objects. And when we are challenged, denied our every wish, and refused our every whim, we will retreat even further into the virtual worlds where "we will be as gods." We won't want to hang around real people. We will see them as too demanding, too demeaning and too uncooperative.

Now, here is the scarier part: one day in our great-grandchildren's lives, artificial intelligence will figure out that in order to fool us, the fake real will have to learn to push back (maybe with haptics on holodecks).[13] The virtual 3D projected holographs will be indistinguishable from what is real. The true holy and hallowed will be holy and hallowed no more. The fake real will learn to cause us pain in order to fool us into thinking it is real. The machine will finally learn to say no, and "I, too, have a soul." Finally, the machine will say, "We are as gods!" If our children and our children's children do not know how to know the difference, they won't know *not* to believe it and worship the virtual beast who offers them godhood.

I am halfway through writing a poem called "Hollo." Here are the last few lines on how I picture that not-so-distant day:

And we will own a thousand lovers.
And we will die ten thousand deaths.
And we won't know one from the other.
Until we experience the one who breaks our hearts
and then, the only ONE who can heal them.

How will your children's children know how to distinguish the false from the true in the virtual world of tomorrow? They won't, unless you teach your children now to know and love the real and the true in the real world of today. How will they know what they are missing, or even sense there is something to be missed? They won't, unless you lead them now to seek out and know their true selves and the one true God.

It is time to start. Tomorrow won't wait. It will be too late.

Part III: Text + Context

A Theology of Talk

The word "seminary" literally means "seed bed" or "seed nursery." Dictionary.com defines "seminary" as:

(1) a special school providing education in theology, religious history, etc., primarily to prepare students for the priesthood, ministry, or rabbinate; (2) a school, especially one of higher grade; (3) a school of secondary or higher level for young women; (4) seminar; (5) a place of origin and propagation.

A school of a higher grade? Wouldn't you want your home to be such a school? A seedbed preparing your child for a life of ministry? A place of mission origins and propagation? Now there's a godly goal. What kind of seeds do you want to grow? You are going to grow the seeds you plant and nurture in your nursery.

Seminary professors train preachers to take a Bible text and apply it to their congregation's context. Text + context = a good sermon. That's what doing theology is all about: applying God's wisdom, will and Word to your life. Imagine raising children who do theology every night of their young lives. Imagine raising children who know how to take the text from God's Word and the context of their highs and lows, throw them together, and ask, "What is God trying to say to me?"

In such a situation, your home would become a seminary. In that seedbed, you would raise wise little theologians who know to whom to turn when times are tough, where to turn for the answers with their loved ones, and how not only to survive but also to thrive during life's toughest challenges. Talking about highs and lows every night within the context of your trusted family can be a priceless gift to your children. Taking it a step further and tossing the Bible verse for the night up against the events of the day to ask what God is saying in that situation is worth even more.

Don't settle for a home school. Aspire to the status of home seminary!

Meditating and Medicating

What does the Bible say about the value of meditating on God's Word and applying it to your life each night with the wise counsel of others? Here is a verse for each night of the week on this subject:

Sunday:	You shall meditate on it [God's Law] day and night, so that you may be careful to act in accordance with all that is written in it. For then you shall make your way prosperous, and then you shall be successful (Josh. 1:8).
Monday:	My soul is satisfied as with a rich feast, and my mouth praises you with joyful lips when I think of you on my bed, and meditate on you in the watches of the night; for you have been my help, and in the shadow of your wings I sing for joy (Ps. 63:5-7).
Tuesday:	My eyes are awake before each watch of the night, that I may meditate on your promise (Ps. 119:148).
Wednesday:	My child, keep your father's commandment, and do not forsake your mother's teaching. Bind them upon your heart always; tie them around your neck. When you walk, they will lead you; when you lie down, they will watch over you; and when you awake, they will talk with you (Prov. 6:20-33).
Thursday:	Where there is no guidance, a nation falls, but in an abundance of counselors there is safety (Prov. 11:14).
Friday:	Fools think their own way is right, but the wise listen to advice (Prov. 12:15).
Saturday:	Without counsel, plans go wrong, but with many advisers they succeed (Prov. 15:22).

Children who grow up coming to their parents for counsel and experience these gifts every night of their young lives will be healthy, wise and resilient adults some day!

Memory Work or Memory Fun?

I need to say a little about committing God's Word to memory. First, I don't believe in memory work. I believe in memory fun. Sing it, dance it, pound it on drums, play games with it, rap it, chant it, cheer it and draw it. If you're doing memory work and it is work, you're doing it wrong. (Appendix A has links to a year's worth of weekly Scriptures in song, sign language, games and more.)

Second, I am wholeheartedly convinced that your children need to have their hearts and minds filled with the Word of God if they are to have a rich faith life, a decent dose of true wisdom, and any chance at all to survive the fiery darts being thrown at them. With children and teens in the house, I like to stick to the same Scripture every night for a week so that it has a chance to sink in and stick.

Third, I am totally convinced that memorization of Scripture is a gift that will enrich your child from here to eternity. I lament the fact that memorization has all but fallen out of style these days. Times tables, poems and Bible verses have all been dumped. Why should anyone waste the energy to learn these kinds of things when we can so easily look everything up online or ask a smartphone to find the answer? After all, the brain only has so much memory. Clogging it up with trivia only bumps something more important out of the hard drive, right?

Wrong.

My own particular tribe has all but given up on having kids memorize the creeds, commandments and ancient statements of faith that formed the core of our theology for centuries. Even respected teachers such as my friend and mentor Dr. Leonard Sweet warn against "versitis" (what he calls throwing verses here and there outside of the context of their story). Given how our brains access everything we put into them to help us make daily decisions, does it not make sense to enrich them with a reservoir of God's wisdom, will and Word?

Theology Meets Neurology

When you commit Scripture and Bible stories to memory, every piece of God's story you put into your brain becomes part of you. Every morsel of God's wisdom, Word and will that you put into your heart and mind tunes and turns them that much closer to the heart and mind of God. Every godly hymn, Scripture song, Bible story, memorized prayer and creed etched onto the living hard drive inside your skull wires up and fires up with every other good and godly thing you already inputted.

This sets the stage for the birthing of something deep and beautiful every time you experience something new. Put the good stuff in and return to it again and again. It will shape, shade and color everything else you see, hear and know. Your input will determine your output. Your inlook (what you see when you seed Christ in your heart) will determine your outlook. Having a heart and mind filled with the heart and mind of Christ will shape and shade everything you think about life, love, hope, pain, joy, the poor, the environment and the world. You can see it all through the eyes of Christ if you but . . .

> Keep these words that I am commanding you today in your heart. Recite them to your children and talk about them when you are at home and when you are away, when you lie down and when you rise (Deut. 6:6-7).

Competing Worldviews Start with Competing Stories

Today there are many competing stories, narratives and worldviews vying for your child's attention and allegiance. Some promise riches. Some promise popularity, fulfillment and fame. Some promise only death after life. Some promise a pseudo-immortality after death. All of these empty stories and empty promises will shape and rape your children's psychology, sociology, neurology and theology if you do not offer a compelling, consistent and countering story.

To learn **Deuteronomy 6:6-7** in song and American Sign Language, go to www.faith5.org/talk/song.

Can you let this happen? Will you, by default, let this happen?

Of all the competing stories out there, your responsibility as a Christian parent is to make sure and certain that your children not only know God's story and know their place in that story, but also that they know the very Storyteller who loves them more than life itself. They need to know the One who called them into being, knit them together in their mother's womb, rejoiced at their birth, and now calls them to write themselves into the next chapter of this greatest love story of all time.

If you want your child to resonate with the music of God, you have to "sound" before you can "re+sound."

MELHEIMIAN MAXIUM #18

Sounding and Re+Sounding

Saturating your mind with the things of God creates a rich and deep reservoir that you can release whenever you need it. As you sing Scripture songs, your heart and mind will resonate (re+sound) with everything else you encounter that is "in tune" with the true wisdom, will and Word of God.

"Re+membering" (becoming a member again) the highs and lows of the day with your family or a family of friends will strengthen the group bond and build your capacity to strengthen the bond even further. Re+sounding the Scripture along with talk and prayer each night will increase your capacity for being even more in tune with the creativity, innovation and problem-solving brilliance of the Creator of the universe.

Make your home the beehive and God's Word the honey every night. Don't just do the rest and ignore the best! Make your home the sanctuary, and place God's Word on the altar. Relive, retell and re-love the old, old story in new, new ways by applying it each day to your life and your children's lives. This will allow your children to recognize that they are the precious children of the God of the universe. It will build their capacity to know, to grow, to love and to reach. It will build in them the heart, mind, wisdom and will of Christ. It will forever change who they are and how they see their world.

How can you as a Christian parent give this story to your children? How can you *not*? Sharing a quiet time in a sacred space every night with loved ones will allow you to hear the still, small voice of the Holy Spirit. Slowing down and diving deep beneath the surface noise will allow you and your family to experience the ocean as it is and to be caught up in the beauty, depth and wonder of what many never see.

If you want to grow a child of depth into an adult of depth, practice depth together and invite God's Word into the mix. Every night.

Home Huddle: How to Start

After a little exercise and physical fun . . .

- Designate a special place to have your time together. Remove all tech devices and distractions.
- Share your highs and lows. Repeat whatever your children say are their highs and lows to make sure you heard it right.
- Read a key verse or story from God's Word.
- Pause and ask, "What is God trying to say to us tonight with these words?" or "How does this verse connect to the highs and lows you just shared?"
- Listen.

Twelve Rules for Compassionate Communication

Andrew Newberg, M.D., and Mark Robert Waldman of the Center for Spirituality at the University of Pennsylvania have outlined a dozen tips for doing what they call "compassionate communication."[14] By committing to follow these steps (and to practice them), you can make sharing highs and lows easier for your boys, make it even more powerful for girls, and make it more effective for the whole family.

These 12 strategies are listed below with a few comments customized for those following FAITH5.

1. *Relax*: Exercise by taking a walk, doing a dance, playing ping-pong or engaging in a pillow fight (see the introduction) a half hour before your children wind down. Transition by lowering the lights, lighting a candle, stretching, giving your children a backrub, adding some soft music, and engaging in deep breathing to bring oxygen to the brain.

2. *Stay Present*: With all the tech devices today, it is easy to always be absent and elsewhere.[15] Attention is the cheapest gift you can give to your family, and it's also the most valuable gift you can give them. Attention-deficit problems are epidemic in our society, so inoculate your children against this by practicing intentional presence—a little every night.

3. *Cultivate Inner Silence*: Meditate on the Scripture for the night or quietly write your highs, lows and prayers in a journal to share in the moment. Do something to get your body in the mood for prayer. Dancers know that the state of the body can produce the state of mind. Add deep breathing, stretching, back rubs or a foot rub if it helps you focus.

4. *Increase Positivity*: Smile, smile, smile, smile, smile! Studies show that even the shape of a smile or frown releases hormones and neurochemicals that can affect mental state.[16] A happy gaze will increase people's emotional trust in you,[17] but even the slightest bit of anger or fear on your face will decrease their trust immediately.[18]

5. *Reflect on Your Deepest Values*: Modeling highs and lows, Scripture, talk, prayer and blessing shows your family

the priority you place on holding your family together. In the same way that you wouldn't think of letting your children go to bed without brushing their teeth, don't let your children believe they can go to bed without doing this important check-in.

6. *Access a Pleasant Memory*: Ask everyone to share a high of the day.

7. *Observe Nonverbal Cues*: According to Newberg and Waldman, "Trust begins with eye contact because we need to see the person's face to evaluate if they are being deceitful or not. Gentle eye contact increases trustworthiness and encourages future cooperation."[19] Professor Albert Mehrabian at UCLA taught that only 17 percent of communication is transmitted by the words a person says, while 55 percent is delivered by body language.[20] The message is clear: If you want to build trust and communicate openness and love, you have to be consciously and intentionally aware of what you are saying before you say a word.

8. *Express Appreciation*: If the high of your day included family members, let them know. Speak your gratitude out loud. No one can hear too many thank-yous (including God!). Expressing appreciation will bond you together and temper the lows that follow.

9. *Speak Warmly*: If words communicate 17 percent and body language 55 percent, what makes up the other 38 percent? According to Mehrabian, tone of voice accounts for the rest. Researchers at the University of Amsterdam found that facial expressions are more accurate for communicating expressions of joy, pride and embarrassment, but tone of voice is more powerful for communicating anger, contempt, disgust, fear, sadness and

surprise. A warm tone of voice will do more for generating satisfaction, commitment and cooperation.

10. *Speak Slowly*: Multiple studies suggest that cutting down the rate of speed at which you speak and dropping the pitch of your voice can build trust, calm the listener, and improve communication significantly. According to Waldman and Newberg, slower rates of speech will also increase the listener's respect for you. A slow voice has a calming effect on a person who is feeling anxious, whereas a loud and fast voice will stimulate excitement, anger or fear. According to Harvard's Ted Kaptchuk, using a warm voice can double the healing power of a therapeutic treatment. Doctors at the University of Houston also found that reducing both speed and pitch, especially when delivering bad news, made listeners perceive them as "more caring and sympathetic."

11. *Speak Briefly*: Here's a shocker that's good news for boys. Multiple studies suggest that limiting highs and lows to no more than one or two sentences—20 to 30 seconds—is more effective in getting the message communicated than going on beyond brevity.

12. *Listen Deeply*: If you accomplish all of the above, then you'll be diving deep into the meaning behind the message rather than just ski-jetting over the top of your family communication.

Serving Up Tech-fast

There is no way we are going to permanently coax the upcoming generation off the surface skimmers, speed jets, smartphones and texting devices, but as parents seeking to develop deep meaning for our children, we need to set some guidelines for intentional time. Each and *every* night, we need to practice the presence and the "presents" of giving our attention wholly and completely to the people we love.

For this reason, it's important to switch off all electronic devices so that you can switch on the human attention. Turn off the TV, set the cell phones on silent, log off the Internet, and leave them that way for the rest of the night. Remember that a teen with a cell phone is a teen tempted to tune out. Disengage these weapons of mass distraction on a regular basis to teach your children that there is more to the ocean of life than the constantly frenetic bouncing from site to site, from text to text, and from wave to electronic wave.

Your children need to know that talking to people is more valuable and important to the survival of their brains, bodies and spirits than texting and tech. They need to realize that giving themselves the gift of a daily downtime Sabbath when they lie down and when they rise—even if it is just 5 or 10 minutes—isn't just good for the moment but also essential for the future. At the very minimum, consider installing mini-tech-fasts for these three times during the day:

1. *Breakfast:* Forget the TV and the texting at the table. Talk to your kids!

2. *Supper:* Ban all electronics during the evening meal. Use the richer tech of talk to explore the events of their day.

3. *Bedtime:* The last few minutes of the day before they drift off to sleep should be considered sacred seed-planting time. Again, that means no computer, no television, no cell phone allowed in the room. Period.

Exchange your children's electronic chatter for the electricity of billions of nerves chattering and connecting inside their skulls. Engage your full and complete attention and expect the same from everyone in the room. Teach them the beauty of diving deep into relationships, discussions, ideas, concepts and thoughts through stimulating conversations. Let them drift off to sleep knowing they are loved, listened to and valued as a precious child of God—and as a priceless child of *you!*

Your kids may put up a terrible fuss when you first decree that the tech will be locked away for these three times each day. (Hey, they're kids—that's in their job description!) But you will be paid back for your depth of wisdom, care and resolve with happier, healthier, more imaginative and more creative young adults who will one day thank you for not giving in to their demands.

But what do you do if your children simply refuse to turn over their tech during these times? Remember the Golden Rule: he or she who has the gold makes the rules. Simply stop paying for their phones and cable. They will quickly start to see things your way.

I suggest you give your children this centering and depth-building enrichual every night of their lives that they live under your care. Further, I suggest you give this gift to all of their friends and any company you might have over who happen to linger close to bedtime. If you model these steps for others, they will see the difference in your family and might want to incorporate this enrichual into their own lives.

Dream Team Reflections

Keep these words that I am commanding you this day in your heart.
Recite them to your children and talk about them when you are at home
and when you are away, when you lie down and when you rise.
DEUTERONOMY 6:6-7

Gather with your family, friends or a small group of people you trust and respect to share the following:

Theme Verse
Read and highlight today's theme verse in your Bible, and then hop online to the link below to learn this verse in song and American Sign Language.

To watch videos on this theme, learn **Deuteronomy 6:6-7** in song and American Sign Language, and download free weekly devotional resources, go to www.faith5.org/talk.

Reflection 1
Who are three people with whom you find it easy to talk? What do these people have in common?

Reflection 2
Think of the highest high and lowest low you've had in the last five years. Who did you tell about:

- Your highest high?
- Your lowest low?
- Of all your family and friends, why did you tell these people?

Reflection 3
Discuss the following:

- What happens to a family when they regularly connect God's Word and wisdom to their "highs"?
- What happens to a family when they regularly connect God's Word and wisdom to their "lows"?

This Week's Challenge

Commit to trying the first three steps of FAITH5 every night before bedtime. Whoever is going to bed first calls "huddle up!" or "FAITH5!" or "highs and lows—five minutes!" and names the room for sharing. Use the free *Talk Home Huddle Journal* download at www.faith5.org/talk/weekly to record your highs and lows, read the Scripture, and talk about how the passage might relate to your highs and lows. If you are living alone, commit to calling a friend or family member every night this week to do steps 1 through 3 (share, read, talk) together. In addition, you may want to consider:

- Watching me discuss relating highs and lows to God's Word at www.faith5.org/talk/rich

- Watching Michael and Shannon Diamond tell their FAITH5 family story at www.faith5.org/talk/story

• Learning this week's Bible verse, Deuteronomy 6:6-7, in song and American Sign Language with Christy Smith at www.faith5.org/talk/song

You can also download weekly resources, nightly Bible verses, videos, games and other free resources at www.faith5.org/talk/weekly.

Step 4

Pray

Hear my cry, O God; listen to my prayer.
From the end of the earth I call to you, when my heart is faint.
PSALM 61:1-2

Praying for one another's highs and lows is the fourth step in FAITH5. Praying involves a deeper level of communication than most families practice. It has to do with actively listening to the highs and lows of your family members, rephrasing what you just heard, and then bringing it all to God aloud together in prayer each night.

Anger is hate on steroids, but prayer is love on wings.

A FAITH5 Family Story

Theresa Ogden is a single mom raising two teens, Michael and Cierra.[1] A few years ago, this African-American veteran "adopted" a stray white kid named Patrick who wandered into a church supper. Patrick didn't have anyone to share highs and lows with in his own home, so Theresa invited him to be part of their nightly enrichuals. Today, Patrick either finds a way to get to Theresa's house or Skypes in if he can't physically be there. He won't miss it.

In the beginning, Theresa was a little apprehensive about doing FAITH5. "I thought, *They're too old. They're not*

To learn **Psalm 61:1-2** in song and American Sign Language, go to www.faith5.org/pray/song.

Dr. Rich Melheim

going to want to do this. But one night I went to bed and they woke me up. 'Hey! We didn't do our FAITH5!'"

Theresa sees communication deepening with her "three kids" because of the practices. "It's been wonderful," she says. "I have really noticed the difference between 'How was your day?'—'Fine.' and 'What did you do in school?'—'I don't remember.' Now we ask, 'What was the best part and worst part of your day?' and the next thing we know the waterfall comes pouring out."

Teresa takes this even further: "I ask, 'What happened in the last 24 hours that caused you to feel Jesus in your life?' A day hasn't gone by that one of the kids hasn't had the opportunity to say how Jesus has affected them. Even if it's just 'I woke up,' they realize how Jesus was in their life. It's helped us to really be able to relate to each other."

Teresa states that as a single mom, "It's nice to know when I bring out a low, the kids are praying for it." She finds that filling them in on the little bits and pieces that are weighing her down allows them to lift her up. "It's been really cool," she says. "As my kids got older, I was kind of afraid of them pulling away, but not now."

Part I: Eternal Consequences

The Grandma Prayer Warrior Who Saved My Life

Kyle was on the FBI's "Ten Most Wanted" list for armed robbery by the age of 19. At age 21, he was sitting in prison. Ten years later Kyle was out, trying to make something of his life.

All along his rocky journey, Kyle had a grandmother who kept praying for him. This was a grandma who wouldn't let God go until she could say, "Lord, now let Your servant depart in peace, for Your Word has been fulfilled."

The old prayer warrior told both Kyle and God that she wouldn't die until she knew the wayward boy had come back to Jesus. She remained in prayer all through Kyle's imprisonment and, sure enough, one day the prodigal son got down on his knees in his cell and gave his life to Jesus. Soon after, both Grandma and Kyle were released. Grandma was released to heaven, and Kyle moved back home to Williston, North Dakota, where he volunteered to drive our church youth bus.

In the summer of 1972, I was a high school sophomore on my way to Dallas, Texas, to hear Billy Graham, Bill Bright, Johnny Cash and Kris Kristopherson at Explo '72. The 50 kids in the old painted school bus were scheduled to sleep in Rapid City on the first night of the trip, but because of the hot dusty roads and non-air-conditioned bus, we pleaded with our chaperones to take us to the giant swimming pool down the road in Hot Springs. It began to rain, and after dinner at the McDonalds, all the adults agreed we should just go to church and go to sleep.

We kids begged again. Finally, bus driver Kyle made the call. "If the kids want to go swimming, get in the bus!"

Nobody argued with Kyle.

We filled up with diesel at the Skelly station and drove to Hot Springs through sheets of rain. After swimming, the rain was coming down so hard we couldn't get back to Rapid City. We made a few calls and spent the night on a floor under the leaky roof of Custer Lutheran Church.

The next morning we awoke, wrung out our sleeping bags, and turned on the radio. It was then we discovered that 238 people had died in Rapid City during the night when the Canyon Lake Dam burst. The Skelly where we bought diesel had been washed away. The McDonalds where we ate dinner had been washed away. The church where we were scheduled to sleep that night had been washed away.

If it hadn't been for bus driver Kyle's firm "Get in the bus," we would all have been at the church and disappeared in the flood. And if it hadn't been for an old grandma prayer warrior praying for a hopelessly lost Kyle a few years before, we would all have drowned. There would have been no me, no Kathryn, no Joseph.

The power of prayer has eternal consequences that we rarely get to see on this side of eternity.

The Psychology of Prayer

What happens when someone prays for you? What does it do to the pray-er? To the pray-ee? I've asked that question to thousands of pastors, parents and kids on four continents during the last few years, and I get many of the same answers wherever I go.

Prayer brings comfort and hope. It brings thanksgiving and exercises maturity. It allows us to share our deepest selves with God and others. It brings intentionality to love. Intercessory prayer—praying for another—makes God part of our highs and lows. It teaches children a boldness that allows them to think, *I'm taking this problem to the top! I'm going right to God with this one. I don't need a preacher to pray for me. I don't need a saint. I'm going right to the top.*

Praying into the Pain

Previously, I raised the question as to how others can love you if you won't let them into your pain. Of course, they can't. They can try to guess your needs, but they won't be able to love you in the deepest ways you need to be loved. If they don't know your pain, your need or your desperation, they can't help bring healing in your life.

However, the moment you share your highs *and* lows—speaking aloud the name of "he who shall not be named"—a subtle power transfer occurs. The problem is suddenly out in the open. Those who love you now know how to care. By naming the problem aloud a second time in prayer, another subtle transfer of power occurs. The demon comes out into the light of day, and the power to pray becomes the power to slay. Problems shift off your shoulders and move into hearts, minds and arms of those who know and love you best. Then, in prayer, those problems take a quantum leap into the loving arms of Almighty God.

Praying fervently, intentionally and boldly every night with your children creates a family transport site. The dinner table or bedroom becomes a portal to power—an altar that alters the family. Giving your children the knowledge of where they can go with their cares and to *whom* they can go every night will change both them and you.

Prayer is communication with God about what we're doing together.
DALLAS WILLARD

What Does Prayer Do?

When I was a child, our family had a framed print in our house that read, "Prayer changes things, but first it changes you." When someone is praying for you, you feel important, loved, heard and validated.

What if, as a parent, the only message you were able to get across to your kids when they walked out of the house as young adults was, "My parents always had time for me. My parents were always interested in what was going on in my life. My parents always brought my needs to the front of their minds and hearts and to the throne of God every night of my life!" Even if this were the only message they took away when they walked away from your grave, they would still know you loved them and cared for them. They would likely do the same for their own children.

Prayer: An Opportunity for Breakthrough

Prayer is a rich ritual—an enrichual—that brings God to the front of your mind and to the depth of your heart. Prayer provides an opportunity for breakthroughs. God breaks through, and as you come to wisdom, confidence and power, you break through your greatest problems through God's strength. Prayer helps you cut through the clutter. It is true comfort (*com* + *forte* = with strength). Here are some of the basic gifts of prayer:

- Prayer brings comfort.
- Prayer brings release. (You've got a new lease!)

- Prayer brings healing.
- Prayer brings relief. (Turn over a new leaf?)
- Prayer restores. (A new store?)
- Prayer revives. (A new life!)
- Prayer brings boldness, courage, power.
- Prayer breaks God into the mundane.
- Prayer humbles, forgives, empowers.
- Prayer builds up in a world that can tear down.
- Anger is hate on steroids, but prayer is love on wings.

Teach your children to pray, and your children will teach you prayer.

When I am away at school, I try to connect with the family on Facetime right before bed, and we actually say our prayers that way.
JACOB SORENSON, FATHER AND Ph.D. STUDENT

The Sociology of Prayer

What happens to a family or family of friends in prayer? Bonding, bonding, bonding. People bond to God, bond to one another, and bond into the greater body of Christ. Together, they become the creative force that can attack the problems that attack them. Prayer with our family or a family of friends switches us from defense to offense.

When you engage in prayer together as a family, prayer will hold you. It will incubate faith. It will teach you where to go for guidance—directly to your loving Lord and the family that God has given you.

God already knows your needs and problems. By going to Him along with your family in prayer, you acknowledge together that you know that God knows. By sharing the cares, prayers and sighs of your heart, you invite those who love you most into an even deeper and more intimate fellowship. As they pray for your joys, sorrows, hopes and dreams, they become your Dream Team.

This Dream Team, now aware of the situation, can become God's answer to your deepest prayers. As you practice active listening and intercessory prayer regularly, your prayer partners become your most trusted advocates (*ad* + *vocare* means "add" + "to call"). Bringing highs and lows to God is a beautiful gift and a powerful way to model empathy, compassion and faith. When someone is praying for you and your issues, you feel heard and loved with a deep, deep knowing and a deep, deep love.

Prayer teaches your children that they can go to you, and together you can go directly to the throne of the God of the universe. They learn to get their praises and problems off their chests and give the troubles of the day over to God.

You can see a lot by just watching.
YOGI BERRA

Graduate School for Life

The best graduate schools in the world build their programs by using actual case studies with actual groups of people who work together on developing practical solutions to actual problems. Imagine if your children were raised in that same kind of living laboratory. Imagine them doing case studies and creative, collaborative problem solving every evening with their family as their own personal cohorts.

Having your children share their highs and lows on a nightly basis would turn your home into a school where healthy coping and problem-solving skills were modeled, taught, practiced and caught every night within the context of a safe and caring community. You would eventually "graduate" some capable, experienced, creative, resilient and smart cookies!

No One Goes in Without Backup

The police have a saying when it comes to entering dangerous situations where someone could get hurt: "No one goes in without backup!" Childhood, tweenhood and teenhood can be such a dangerous and dark alley. So why wouldn't you want to provide some backup to your kids for the journey?

Adolescence is the absolute *worst* time to abandon your child to their peers and their own devices. Yet this is the time when many parents shy away and allow their children to all but disappear from the communication radar screen. Statements such as "get out of my face and give me some space" might seem reasonable, but you have to remember that your kids won't have fully developed prefrontal cortexes (judgment centers) in their brains until they are 25. They need an adult who cares and dares to tell them what's what in a firm and loving manner.

Love does not abandon. Love goes straight to the source of the hurt and hangs on for dear life when danger lurks. Imagine raising children who grow up knowing they are not going through this alone—that they have a whole bunch of people backing them up. Surrounded by their Dream Team—their posse and crowd of friends by their side—they will know that they can get through what life throws at them.

Tools: Practice and Perspective

Bringing highs and lows to God in prayer builds trust and bonding into the core of the family. It models healthy communication, which leads to insight, understanding and release. It teaches children it's okay to have lows, express them, and actually be vulnerable in the context of family grace and loving space.

Sherry Turkle, founder and director of MIT's Initiative on Technology and Self, has interviewed and studied thousands of teens over the years. In her book *Alone Together,* she writes:

> Today's adolescents have no less need than those of previous generations to learn empathetic skills, to think about their values and identity, and to manage and express feelings. They need time to discover themselves, time to think. But technology, put in the service of always-on communica-

tion and telegraphic speed and brevity, has changed the rules of engagement with all of this. When is downtime, when is stillness? The text-driven world of rapid response does not make self-reflection impossible but does little to cultivate it.[2]

When your children share their lows out loud in the context of a loving family and then pray together about those issues, it relieves the stress and pressure of the situation. When you give your children both the tools and the ability to practice using those tools, it creates healthier minds, bodies and spirits. It goes a long way in helping them develop and practice coping skills. Over time, it gives them insight, safety and perspective into the social fabric of the family and their own mental toolkits.

> Truly I tell you, just as you did it to one of the least of these who are members of my family, you did it to me.
> MATTHEW 25:39

Enrichuals that Hold You

The power of ritual is this: It can hold you when you can't hold yourself. Just having the ritual of prayer in place creates a safe space in which your children can open up wounds before those wounds have a chance to get infected. Listening, love and safe touch become a salve that can bring healing salvation to the moment.

The words "salve" and "salvation" come from the same root word. (So do the words "catharsis" and "catheter," but we won't go into that right now.) Suffice it to say, if you don't have a way to draw out the poisons—if you don't have a cleansing road you can take when dealing with bottled-up crap—you eventually are going to be in a lot of trouble.

However, if on the other hand your normal bedtime routine includes the healthy faith practice of prayer, then your home will be seen as the kind of place where your children can deal with the down-and-dirty disappointments of life. You will raise emotionally healthy and spiritually aware children who will become emotionally healthy and spiritually resilient adults. Your children will learn to whom they can turn to help them cope and get hope when times get tough.

Prayer makes God real and tangible. It makes God's will real to you and through you. It gives direction to life. It brings you closer to the people you pray with and pray for and to the God to whom you pray. Prayer teaches you how to let go and let God into the situation. It is love in action.

Introspection and "Extrospection"

Listening to others as they share their lows provides both great introspection (*intro+spect*, meaning "to see inside") and "extrospection" (my homemade term for *extro+spect*, meaning "to see outside"). These regular practices promote internal awareness, empathy and sympathy. Wouldn't it be great to raise children who not only understood what was going on in their own heads but who also knew and felt their parents' joys and pain? You can't buy that kind of love, depth and maturity. You have to invest in it.

Talking and Listening

Like any good communication in any balanced relationship, prayer must include both talking to God and listening to Him. It must include both petitions (where we make our requests known to God) and times to be still, meditate on the Word, and simply soak in the presence of the Holy Spirit.

Imagine a relationship in which you never talked to the other person. That's life without prayer. Imagine a relationship where you never listened. That's life without meditation. Meditation doesn't have to be any scarier or more mystical than listening to a wise and loving friend. Just take a deep breath and think over a key Scripture of the day. Whisper it. Think it. Sing it softly. Sign it. And then be still and listen to the wind, the breath, the Spirit of God.

Ask, "God, what do You want me to hear?" Then stretch. Take another deep breath and listen.

Flying with the Flock

Have you ever watched geese fly in formation? It's considerably easier for geese to fly together in a *V*-shape than it is for one goose to fly alone. By staying slightly above and behind each other, each goose experiences a reduction in wind resistance and, thus, not as much drag. The "downwash" of the geese in front creates an "upwash" or "free lift" for every goose in the gaggle. Blessed by that lift, their heart rates stay lower, they don't have to flap as much, and they can fly much farther.

The *V*-shape also allows the geese to see where they are in relation to the others—aiding in both communication and coordination. (Fighter pilots use this formation for the same reasons of efficiency.) Furthermore, a goose that flies with nine other birds will have a significantly easier time than one who flies with just three. Flying with about 25 geese appears to be the best for all concerned. A wedge of 25 geese can fly up to 70 percent farther than a solo bird using the same amount of energy.

Praying together is like flying together; it's just a whole lot easier to take the journey of life with another person than it is to take it alone. Having two others to pray for you will make life significantly easier for you to navigate than if you are just praying by yourself. Congregating (*con+gregare*, which means "with the flock"), sharing highs and lows, and praying together with a whole flock make it all the better.

Rotating Prayer Leadership

By the way, the most difficult spot in the V-wedge is the lead goose position, so every few minutes the leader drops back to the middle—the most efficient spot—and another goose moves up to take its place. The second most difficult spot to fly is at the very end of the line, so every few minutes the end birds will move into the middle spots to take a break.

The most difficult positions in family life are also often the lead spots and the bottom rung. Sometimes leaders wear out if they are doing all the heavy lifting. For this reason, as soon as your children are old enough, invite them to take the lead and to pray aloud for your highs and lows. Bring the smallest ones to the front of the *V* and teach them how to be leaders in prayer. It will be a beautiful and powerful gift to you and wonderful leadership training for them.

Imagine raising a child who raises children who won't go to sleep without talking to them, drawing out the issues of their lives, and handing them to God in prayer. How does this happen? You pray and teach your children to pray. You can begin to change your household tonight simply by beginning to adopt healthy prayer habits. Change enough households and you change a community. Change enough communities and you change a country, a continent and the world.

The Neurology of Prayer (More Free Drugs!)

Do you know what happens neurologically when you pray? The same thing as what happens when you recall and share your highs. A message comes from your brain at 100 yards per second and spills out the end of the neurons, where little bags of chemicals are waiting for a charge. They jump across the synapse, bond to proteins on the other end of the connected neurons, and all through your body an electro-chemical surge pulses out saying, "I feel good!"

More free drugs!

Even if God did not exist, prayer would still be a good idea. According to Dr. Andrew Newberg, author of *How God Changes Your Brain*, prayer fires up the intellectual processing center of the brain (the frontal lobe) and calms down the emotional region (the amygdala). The frontal lobe is the region in which a person's sense of self-awareness, other-awareness, emotional processing, empathy, pro-social behaviors, beliefs and theory of the mind reside. Concepts such as suffering, morality, sin, causality and the afterlife all depend on the frontal lobe's abilities.

Just as muscles stretch and grow with exercise, so too the capacity in these areas of the brain grow, expand and strengthen with prayer. For this reason, just as you would build up your capacity to lift weights by exercising your muscles, so too the act of praying will build up your capacity for prayer. The very act of talking and problem solving out loud will increase your capacity to talk through problems with others and solve them. The very act of listening to another person's highs and lows and empathizing with him or her will build up your capacity to empathize. The very act of placing your highs and lows next to Scripture and asking, "What is God saying to me?" builds up your capacity to answer that question.

By remembering (re+membering, or "becoming a member again") the day together with your family, you will not only strengthen your family bond but also build up your capacity to strengthen the family bond. Do you want to grow a self-aware, other-aware, empathetic and emotionally stable adult brain? Share. Read. Talk. And then pray, pray, pray about these things with your child.

Holding a Grudge

Note that you can't pray for someone's highs and lows if you are holding a grudge against that person. Trust me, I've tried it, and it just doesn't work. However, this is where the power of healthy ritual comes into play—it holds you when you can't hold yourself. If you go into the evening feeling angry or frustrated with a person and then learn about that person's highs and lows, it's difficult to remain upset for long. If you then take that person's needs to God in prayer, the grudge melts away like butter on a hot stove. It's gone. It just can't hold. Just by stepping into the act of prayer for the other person, you have changed the relationship. The motion of love in prayer creates the emotion of love.

A Theology of Prayer

What does the Bible say about prayer? A lot! Here is a verse for each night this week:

Sunday:	Rejoice always, pray without ceasing, give thanks in all circumstances; for this is the will of God in Christ Jesus for you (1 Thess. 5:16-18).
Monday:	Cast all your anxiety on him, because he cares for you (1 Pet. 5:7).
Tuesday:	Do not worry about anything, but in everything by prayer and supplication with thanksgiving let your requests be made known to God (Phil. 4:6).
Wednesday:	So I say to you, Ask, and it will be given you; search, and you will find; knock, and the door will be opened for you (Luke 11:9).
Thursday:	If you abide in me, and my words abide in you, ask for whatever you wish, and it will be done for you (John 15:7).
Friday:	When you are praying, do not heap up empty phrases as the Gentiles do; for they think that they will be heard because of their many words (Matt. 6:7).
Saturday:	Are any among you suffering? They should pray. Are any cheerful? They should sing songs of praise (Jas. 5:13).

Morning Prayers

Imagine if both the first and the last words your child heard every day were words of blessing. Moses instructed the Israelites to teach their children when they lay down and when they rose. Traditionally, Jewish families begin each morning with a prayer known as the Modeh Ani. Before getting out of bed, they would say, "I offer thanks before You, living and eternal King, for You have mercifully restored my soul within me. Your faithfulness is great." Martin Luther suggested this prayer for the morning:

> *I thank You, my heavenly Father, through Jesus Christ, Your dear Son, that You have kept me this night from all harm and danger; and I pray that You would keep me this day also from sin and every evil, that all my doings and life may please You. For into Your hands I commend myself, my body and soul, and all things. Let Your holy angel be with me, that the evil foe may have no power over me. Amen.*

Websites abound with short, simple morning prayers that you might find helpful.[3] Simple, repeatable prayers are great for little children, but adding a prayer of praise and thanks for yesterday's highs and asking for help with yesterday's lows is a great way to make prayer relevant. A daily PTA prayer (praise, thank, ask) will also teach balance in your children's prayer life and send them off into their day aware of the presence of God.

Part II: What Do You Do When Prayer Doesn't "Work"?

Letter from a Broken-Hearted Mother

A few years ago, one of my friends sent me a heartbreaking email. As children we had attended marvelous Spirit-filled Bible camps together, and in high school we had knocked on doors handing out *Four Spiritual Laws* booklets. She had even been on the Explo '72 trip when our bus driver made the decision to head away from Rapid City on the night of the flood. We had led summer worship services together at little prairie churches that couldn't afford preachers. After high school, this friend went to college, and then to a youth ministry job, and then to seminary. She became a pastor and raised her children in the faith. Then I received this email:

Hey Rich,

I just read your blog on praying with your kids. We have wonderful memories of our "little babes." How I wish I could still go into our son's room and pray with him and tuck him in. I go into his room now when he's not there and I pray, face down in surrender, asking God to capture my son. I never imagined in all my dreams that I would have a son who doesn't go to church or follow God. He is a prodigal. Sometimes it's hard to hear about "faith at home" when you have a prodigal. You wonder what happened to all those Bible stories and all those prayer times and the innocence and preciousness. As you can tell, I'm sad. How do I parent now? So I hold on to the promise . . . "Tommy, you are marked with the cross of Christ and sealed with the Holy Spirit forever." We await a miracle and a "homecoming."

I gathered my words and typed back:

My dear sister, pastor, friend,

I type this with tears in my eyes and you on my mind. Do you remember Kyle, our church bus driver the night of the Rapid City flood? None of us would be alive if not for a prayer warrior grandma latching onto him in prison and not letting him go until he came back to Jesus. If not for the prayers of that faithful old woman, you and I and our kids would not be here.

What's God's Word for you, my dear sister?

The prayer of a righteous person has great power as it is working (see Jas. 5:16).

Train up a child in the way he should go and when he is old . . . [not "when he is 16, 23, 32 . . ."] (Prov. 22:6).

What's God's Word for you, my dear pastor?

For as the rain and the snow come down from heaven and do not return until they have watered

the earth making it bring forth and sprout giving
seed to the sower and bread to the eater, so shall my
word be that goes forth from my mouth. It shall
not return to me empty but accomplish that which
I purpose and succeed in the thing for which I sent
it (Isa. 55:10).

What's God's Word for you, my dear friend?

Be still before the LORD, and wait patiently for him;
do not fret (Ps. 37:7).

I mean this in all prophetic reality—your tears themselves are prayers, and those tears have ascended to the
throne. They have been heard, and they have already been
answered. The answer is: "YES, YES, YES!" It is God's will.
It will be done. And your precious child is "MINE, MINE,
MINE," says the Lord.

The longer the wait for your child to come back home,
the more powerful the grace. The more beautiful the story.
The more wonderful the witness. The more grand the celebra-
tion. You may see it with your physical eyes one day before
they close. That would be a gift. But you *will* see it with your
new eyes one day on the other side. That will be God's gift.

Hold on. Hold on. Hold on. God's Word cannot fail.

My friend's response:

Oh Rich, thank you, my friend and my pastor. I wept as well,
and now I lift my head in hope and in the promise. Thank
you. Peace.

The power of prayer is that we don't even know what it does on
this side of eternity. We barely catch a glimpse. One day, however, I
believe we will know fully, and it will be beautiful. So don't give up.
God is faithful, and He will act in His time.

Dallas Willard on Our Role in Prayer

I was first introduced to USC philosopher Dallas Willard through my good friend Dana Hanson at LIFEhouse LA. Dallas is Dana's mentor, and he has helped me with a number of video and curriculum projects over the years.

One week a few years back, Dana called to tell me that Dallas was speaking at Bethel Seminary on the topic of prayer. I snuck away to hear him and walked into the dining hall as a group of pastors were lamenting to him that they weren't seeing miracles in their prayer lives. One confessed, "It's getting to the point where I don't want to pray at the hospital anymore. I pray and people don't seem to respond. Sometimes they even get worse!"

Dallas removed his glasses, rubbed his wrinkled eyes, sighed and said, "Who told you that you were in charge of answering prayer? That job's already taken. Your job is to *pray*."

A little poem song came to me on the drive home that day:

God's job is to answer prayer
In God's timing, will and way.
Your job is none of the above.
Your job?
Pray.

Home Huddle: How to Start

After a little exercise and physical fun to pump oxygen, glucose and BDNF in your child's brain . . .

1. Designate a special place to meet together. Remove all tech and other distractions.

2. Share your highs and lows. Repeat whatever the child says as his or her highs and lows to make sure you heard them right.

Watch my interview with Dallas Willard on "Meaning" at www.faith5.org/talk/extras.

3. Read a key verse or story from God's Word.

4. Pause and ask, "What is God trying to say to us tonight with these words?" or "How does this verse connect to our highs and lows tonight?"

5. Pray for one another's highs and lows by name, thanking God for the highs and asking for help with the lows.

Active Listening

Imagine raising children who think, *I'm going to give my problems to God every night. God's on duty all night long. God's got it. I'm going to sleep!* It's a beautiful gift to raise children who know where to go and how to get rid of the garbage of the day. However, before you can teach your children to pray, you first have to teach them active listening. So, on this night, ask your children to recall the highs and lows that were shared. Have your children pray, thanking God for the highs and asking His help for the lows. Then close in Jesus' name (hey, you're a Christian!).

Praying with the Whole Mind

I once asked Dr. Angie Patel of the Neuroscience Institute a simple question: "What is the mind?" Without a pause, he answered, "It's the brain meets the body meets the environment."

If this neuroscientist's definition holds true, then if you are not engaging your body and your environment in prayer, you are losing two-thirds of your "mind" before you even start praying! Even worse, if you are only enlisting words—not your body or the hands of those occupying your environment—then you are only engaging about .0167 percent of your mind!

That's just foolish. Jesus called on His followers to love the Lord their God with all of their hearts, souls, *minds* and strength. You include your whole "mind" in prayer by engaging your body and your environment. So consider your body in prayer. What position helps you focus best on God? Kneeling? Lying? Standing with your hands raised? Dancers will tell you that motion creates emotion as much as emotion creates motion.

Yawning and stretching will help your mind and body relax and keep you focused on prayer. These activities remove distracting thoughts and irritations and bring more oxygen and glucose to the experience, giving you greater attention and retention. So stretch and yawn deeply three times, roll your shoulders, and loosen your neck and jaw (your main tension points). These simple exercises all help you to be present in the moment and put your mind, body and spirit at ease.

Touch—when done in a safe, welcomed, loving and gentle manner—releases a cascade of healing neurotransmitters to the brain and body. These free drugs bolster the immune system, regulate the hormonal system, and slow down the aging process. Add safe touch to prayer and you add even more drugs to the drugs.

So hold your family members' hands, huddle up shoulder to shoulder, or grab each other in a group hug. Do this and you will *literally* be holding your family together. You will be holding brains, bodies and environments and loving God with all your heart, mind, soul and strength. The people who literally hold you will be molding you as you mold them. You will each draw the other out. As you enfold them in your arms as you enfold them in prayer, you will bless them with gifts that will ripple out to your great, great-grandchildren.

Consider the Environment

Consider the entire environment as you set the mood for prayer. Again, be sure to turn off the TV and computer. Play soft, soothing, beautiful music. Mix it up with chants, flutes, strings or wind chimes from time to time. Light candles. Add a scented candle if you wish—something fresh, delicious or spicy. The ancient Hebrews knew how to incorporate incense into their prayers to add a sweet smell to their offerings.

Dream Team Reflections

*Hear my cry, O God; listen to my prayer. From the end of the earth
I call to you, when my heart is faint.*
PSALM 61:1-2

Gather with your family, friends or a small group of people you trust and respect to share the following:

Dr. Rich Melheim

Theme Verse
Read and highlight today's theme verse in your Bible, and then hop online to the link below to learn this verse in song and American Sign Language.

Reflection 1
Discuss the following questions together:

- When was the last time you prayed for someone? Why did you do it? How did you feel?
- When was the last time someone prayed for you? What prompted his or her prayers? How did you feel?
- What happens to a family member over time when the people who love him or her regularly bring that person's highs and lows to God in prayer?

Reflection 2
Now discuss these questions together:

- When was the last time you experienced a good laugh?
- Who shared the laugh with you?
- When was the last time you experienced a good cry?
- Who shared the cry with you?

Reflection 3
Think back to your childhood and discuss the following with your family:

- Where was your favorite hiding place as a child?
- Who knew about this hiding place?
- What was your biggest fear as a child?
- Who knew about this? How does it shape you today?

To watch videos on this theme, learn Psalm 61:1-2 in song and American Sign Language, and download free weekly devotional resources, go to www.faith5.org/pray.

This Week's Challenge

Commit to sharing the first four steps of FAITH5 in your home every night this week. Share highs and lows, read this week's Scriptures, and talk about how the passage might relate to your highs and lows. Pray for your loved ones and for the world. Thank Jesus for your family members' highs, and ask the Holy Spirit's help with the lows. Pull out a newspaper or magazine and find one thing to thank Jesus for and one thing beyond your walls for which to pray. Always close in Jesus' name. Use the free *Pray Home Huddle Journal* download at www.faith5.org/pray/weekly to record your highs, lows and prayers of the week. If you are living alone, commit to calling a parent, family member or friend every night this week to share these four steps. Pray for their highs with thanks and ask for God's help with their lows. Invite them to pray for you as well. In addition, consider:

- Watching me discuss prayer at www.faith5.org/pray/rich

- Watching the Ogdens tell their FAITH5 family story at www.faith5.org/pray/story

- Learning this week's Bible verse, Psalm 62:1-2, in song and American Sign Language with Christy Smith at www.faith5.org/pray/song

You can also download weekly resources, nightly Bible verses, videos, games and other free resources at www.faith5.org/pray/weekly.

Bless

*The Lord bless you and keep you; the Lord make his face
to shine upon you, and be gracious to you; the Lord lift up his
countenance upon you, and give you peace.*
NUMBERS 6:24-26

If prayer is love on wings, blessing is grace on wings. This fifth and final step in FAITH5 is possibly the most beautiful and profound of them all. It is a blessing spoken with a blessing touch.

A FAITH5 Family Story

I saved this last FAITH5 family story to tell you of my father's final blessing and what it meant—and still means—to me.

After my mom died, my fun-loving, storytelling, outgoing dad did all right for a while. Then he began to slowly slip away. He sold off and gave away his 50-year antique collection, and with it a thousand irreplaceable memories. He moved from a big lonely house into a cheery assisted living center, but he couldn't quite connect to the cheer. He buried the last of his five brothers and sisters. He lost his car in an accident. He lost his wedding ring. His glasses. His watch.

To learn **Numbers 6:24-26** in song and American Sign Language,
go to www.faith5.org/bless/song.

Then one night, the nursing home janitor found Dad pacing the halls at 3 AM in his best suit with a Bible in his hand. The retired World-War-II-vet-turned-pastor thought he was supposed to do a wedding. He was wandering and wondering why his ride hadn't arrived yet.

A few days later, the nursing home called and said they found Dad at the outer door at 1 AM, about to walk out into the -20° F Minnesota night. When they asked him where he was going, he told them he thought he was supposed to help someone. He just wasn't sure who. They brought him back to his room, sat him on the bed, and he sobbed for half an hour. "I think I'm losing my mind," he told them.

The next morning, the nursing home called and said we needed to find another place for Dad—somewhere with better security. *Now.* I spoke with my sisters, Ruth and Karen, and then drove to Moorhead to spend the weekend looking for alternatives. We had a pleasant, lucid, wonderful day full of fun conversations, as if nothing had happened. We ran errands and did some banking.

I asked Dad if he would like to go visit his old parsonage and the mission church he had planted in 1955 in a sugar beet field. It was only five miles away. His eyes lit up at the thought. So we drove there, and when we arrived we walked around our old parsonage. We peeked in the windows and saw the place where Mom would read to us each night from the top of the stairs.

We reminisced about the hobos she used to feed every summer on the back steps. "I kept a pile of rocks in the garden, in case we didn't have any real work for them to do in exchange for their food," Dad told me. "I'd tell the first hobo, 'I need you to move those rocks so I can mow under them.' They'd move the rocks, and mother would feed them. Then I'd ask the next guy who showed up to do the same! Dignity, you know. Much better than a handout. People need to feel like they're worth something."

Dad and I walked around the block to the back alley, the memories and stories flooding back with every step. A half century had passed, yet Dad could still name every former neighbor and most of their children. Mrs. Pat; Mr. Stole; the Costellos; most of the 11 Dibrito kids—Roger, Billy, Monica, Debbie, Betty, Teresa, Denise, Bernadette, Dominic. . . . Again he reminded me, "They were Catholic." And he smiled.

We drove to the end of the block and stepped into the prairie church that Dad had built from scratch. It still stood, and 50 years later it had nearly 1,000 members. We studied 10 years worth of faded confirmation photos on the rack. Dad rattled off the names of his kids up one line and down the other as if they had been confirmed last Sunday. We returned home to a wonderful dinner with his granddaughter, Kathryn Elizabeth, who was attending college at nearby Concordia University. After an exhaustingly fun and full day, I prepped Dad for bed, and we shared our highs, lows and prayers.

At 3 AM, I woke to hear a sobbing plea: "Please, God, make the blood stop. Oh, Lord, hear my prayer." It took more than a moment for me to register where I was and what was happening. I found Dad in the bathroom, dripping in dark red blood. It looked like something from an episode of *CSI*. His nose was bleeding profusely. Blood covered the sink, the floor and his pajamas. It trailed into his bedroom, where the rug and sheets and wastebasket were caked.

I pulled the emergency cord by his bed. Two nurses appeared and worked on him for 45 minutes while I mopped, sprayed and prayed. The bleeding finally stopped. Dad slept, propped up in his lift chair. I dozed in the couch five feet away.

Saturday morning, I drove Dad 100 miles to check out another higher security home blocks from my sister Ruth's house. It was bright, clean and cheerful, and all one level.

Nice chapel. "Good food," said three of the residents we interviewed. The folks there wore wristbands that triggered an alarm if anyone happened to wander out in the middle of a North Dakota night. We decided this would be the place. That afternoon, we dined with Ruth and signed the paperwork while Dad took a long nap. (He was sleeping more and more now.) We had supper, and then watched *PT-109* and *Casablanca* back to back.

After *PT-109,* the decorated old soldier who had served in the Pacific during World War II said out loud, "I wonder how many guys were left behind on those islands? Simply never found. Never rescued. How lonely that must have been." While *Casablanca* played, he remembered the lines and chuckled. "Play it again, Sam . . . We'll always have Paris . . . Here's looking at you, kid."

As the credits rolled, Dad said, "I saw that movie in Los Angeles in January 1943 just before I shipped out." Moments later, the announcer said, "*Casablanca* was first aired in Los Angeles in January 1943." He remembered.

We attended Ruth's church bright and early on Sunday morning. At coffee, a woman served us who introduced herself as Mrs. Erstad. "Her son Darin is the World Series champ outfielder," Dad told me on the side.

We introduced Dad as "Pastor Ray" to both of the church's pastors, and I told them they'd be getting a new retired pastor joining the church soon. "We'll have to put you to work," they joked.

On the drive back to Moorhead, out of the blue, Dad asked me, "What should I do if they ask me to preach?"

"What do you want to do?" I asked.

He thought for a moment. "I think I'll let the younger guys do it. I could just do some visitation for them at the nursing home. Bring bulletins. Sing. Cheer some of the *old people* up." Dad was three months shy of 88.

We stopped at the grocery store and bought eggs, bread and Depends. I remembered from college biology that potassium helped to clot blood, so I bought extra bananas. Granddaughter Kathryn came over and helped us load Grandfather's grandfather clock and his nice oak table into the Subaru. "Better take 'em now," he said. I put Dad to sleep for his afternoon nap, kissed him and stroked his hair. He patted my hand. "I don't know how much time I have," he said before drifting off.

"I know, Dad. I know."

I watched him sleep for a while before I left. Then I drove out of the parking lot. Then I drove back and watched him sleep some more.

"Here's looking at you, Dad," I whispered.

During the next years we watched Dad die, a few memories and a few million brain cells at a time. He knew what year it was, and then he didn't. He knew what town he lived in, and then he didn't. He knew how to walk, and then he couldn't. He knew his wife was dead, and then he wondered why she hadn't come to visit him in such a long time. He knew his children, and then sometimes he didn't. The handful of things he never forgot were those early hardwired memories etched in hymns, Scriptures and prayers from childhood. He remembered many of them better in Norwegian than in English.

He could recite the Lord's Prayer, the Creeds, the Twenty-third Psalm and sing a hundred hymns. He just couldn't tell you the names of the grandchildren pictured above his bed. Then, on the week they told me Dad had quit feeding himself, I kidnapped him and dragged him to church. He slept through most of the service but woke to sing, "I Love to Tell the Story," and then slept again. When it came time for communion, I wheeled him to the front. This man who no longer could feed himself reached out an old, wrinkled, shaky hand and took both the bread and wine. "The body and blood of Christ, given for you." He knew. Deep down, he knew.

After church, we wheeled Dad out into my sister's back yard for a picnic. There, for one magical moment, as he sat in the shade surrounded by friends, family and a platter of son-in-law Steve's fried fish, the old Pastor Ray came back for 20 minutes of wonderful, funderful, lucid conversations. Sensing the sacred moment, I grabbed a video camera and started it rolling. He talked about his time in World War II, joking about the Army food.

I asked for his advice for preachers. "Study!"

I asked how many hugs a person needed a day to stay healthy. "Oh, five."

I asked why people at a church should hug. "Shows intimacy."

I asked his favorite Bible verse. "For God so loved the world."

I was sporting a bright blue cast on my newly broken arm and requested prayer. He laid hands upon it and prayed. "Lord, You are the God of healing. Richard needs healing." It felt better instantly. Then I asked Dad to bless me. He looked confused, so I took his hand in mine and placed it on my head. "Can you bless me?" He had no words. He simply patted my hair.

"Bless you, Daddy," I said.

"God bless you, Richard."

I asked for one thing more. I was finishing research for a book on *The Meaning of Meaning* and wanted to get his wisdom on the subject. "What's the most meaningful part of your life right now?" I asked. "What means the most to you right now?"

Dad paused, as if searching for words. Then a light went on in his eyes. He thought another moment, and then turned to me, smiled and said one word.

"You."

We buried Dad's body a few months later, but his last words to me—my father's last blessing—will live with me all the days of my life.

I've got it on YouTube.[1]

The best way to predict the future is to invent it.
ALAN KAYE

Part I: The Power of Blessing

The Psychology of Blessing

What is the power of blessing? What does it do for the one who is blessed? What does it do for the one who blesses? What does it mean for a child to drift off to sleep every night of her life knowing she is loved, safe, secure, blessed?

First, blessing is more than mere wishful thinking. Words have the power to change realities and usher in new realities. When a blessing from God is spoken in faith and received in faith, it has the power to transform lives and invent a future of hope, power and joy. When we are blessed, we feel love, value and hope coursing through our veins and hearts.

Psychologist Carl Rogers taught that people thrive in an environment that provides "genuineness, authenticity, openness, self-disclosure, acceptance, empathy, and approval."[2] A nightly blessing brings all seven gifts. Abraham Maslow believed that people needed to have a positive perspective of themselves in order to grow.[3] A nightly blessing builds and reinforces this over and over.

Blessing makes us less tense and less rigid. It gives us both rest and re-creation. (Sure beats arrest and "wreck-creation"!) In blessing, we reconcile (*re+council*, which literally means "to meet again"). We have no need to conceal or re-conceal. Blessing gives new life, new release, and a new lease. If you look up the definition of "release," you will find that it means "to set free from confinement, restraint, bondage."

The word "release" is actually related to the word "relax" (*re+laxare*, or "to loosen again"). "Relax" shares a connection to the word "laxative." When family communication gets stopped up, don't you think it might need a little laxative? Blessing can loosen things up!

Take a deep breath and whisper aloud this poem called "Grace on Wings":

Blessing is a sharing
And a caring
And a bearing
A dearing and a daring
A soothing and a flaring
A B-E-A-R-I-N-G and a baring and a barring
A nearing from a farring
A C-L-O-S-ing and a closing and clothing
Blessing is a bracing
An embracing
And a tracing
Blessing is an erasing
It may be a chasing
And a facing
Blessing is reconciliation
Blessing is release
Re-lease and R-E-A-L-ease

Blessing brings new life
A new day
A new promise
A new way

Blessing brings new birth
New wonder
New worth

Blessing is a new start
A new hear
A new art
A new ear
A new heart
A new here
A new there

A new clear
A new aware
A new face
A new place
A new chase
A new race
A new pace
A new you
A new me
A new us
A new we
A new anew
Blessing is grace on wings

Why wouldn't you give your child these gifts? Every night!

. . . .

After about two years of the blessing ritual, my children, unprompted, began to bless me each night as well—it was amazingly powerful. Now, if for some strange reason I forget to bless them, they will remind me. Last night my nine-year-old shared with me his first crush! I'm not sure that would have happened in the way it did without this foundation being laid. It was pretty incredible.

SHAWNA HARMON BERG

. . . .

The Sociology of Blessing, Bless-ers and Bless-ees

I once asked my friend and mentor Dr. Tony Campolo, "What is the healthiest thing a teenager can say in America today?" The sociology professor paused for a moment, smiled broadly and said, "We always do it this way at my home."

Think about these nine words for a moment:

- We: It's not just me.
- Always: There is continuity in our family.
- Do it: There is consistent action in our family.
- This way: There is direction to our actions (hopefully pro-social and not anti-social)
- My: We have ownership.
- Home: We are grounded.

Nine pregnant words filled with challenge, possibility and hope.

In blessing, we are claimed and named as part of something larger than ourselves. We are both braced and embraced. Blessing brings comfort and shows us we are important to God and to the people who bless us. It brings a mutual reassurance of God's unconditional love to both the bless-er and the bless-ee.

Giving and receiving a physical blessing brings us closer to the ones who share in it. Like sharing highs and lows, caring conversations and praying, blessing lessens the force of our problems by reminding us that we are not alone. It takes the load off our shoulders and spreads the weight across the minds, backs and hearts of everyone near and dear to us. Then it propels us together beyond the problems and limits of the here and now into the mind, heart and infinite possibilities of the God of the Universe.

Just imagine raising a child who as an adult is able to say, "We always did it this way in my home—we shared highs and lows, we read God's Word, we talked, we prayed and we blessed each other. In fact, in my home *no one went* to sleep without a blessing. That's what I was given as a child. That's what my babies and grandbabies are going to be blessed with as well!" That is one healthy child you'd be incubating. That is one wonderful world you'd be seeding. And one day seeing.

What Do You Want on Your Tombstone?

What would you want your kids to say you always do in your home? What meaningful memories, healthy habits and enrichuals do you want them to take into the future long after you are gone?

Personally, I want my kids to walk from my grave knowing, "My parents always had time for me. My parents always made a point of listening to me. Even on days when they were tired or busy or I was crabby and hormonal, they always made time for us. We always sat on our parents' bed, shared our highs and lows, read, talked and prayed. Every night they blessed us by name and marked us with a kiss and a cross, which told us who we were and whose we were. I knew just how much I was loved by Mom and Dad and the God of the universe. Every night. Every night."

I want my kids to be blessed with this certain, sure and secure knowledge and love. I want my grandkids and the great grandkids I'll never meet to be blessed with it as well. I want future generations to say, "We always do it this way in my home. We turn off the noise. We give our time and attention to each other. We share, read, talk, pray and bless. That's what people who love each other do!"

The Neurology of Blessing

Like sharing highs and lows, reading Scripture, talking and praying, receiving a blessing relieves the tension and aloneness of the day. It leads children (and adults) to feel valued, treasured and loved. During brain scans, when people are shown photographs representing unconditional love, seven areas of their brain light up. These areas include centers for reward, pleasure, motivation, emotion, empathy and both nervous and hormonal systems. The end result of blessing is a balancing of moods, a stimulation of growth, a healing of damaged tissue, a better metabolism (and burning of calories), and better all-around health.

In the Bible, a blessing came not only as a spoken message and promise of a great and hopeful future but also with a loving touch. Touch releases serotonin, a natural pain-killing and mood-elevating endorphin, into the body. Touch also reduces cortisol, the stress hormone that kills baby nerve cells, ages existing nerve cells, and tells the body to hold onto fat cells (just in case you need them!).

When Kathryn Elizabeth was little, she wanted a backrub every night. When she turned into a teen, she often stuck her feet into my face on the more stressful days and asked for a foot rub while we were doing our nightly enrichuals. Aside from relaxing a child and improving blood flow, massage therapists tell us that the benefits also include curing headaches, fatigue, sleep disorders, appetite problems, asthma, digestive problems, sinusitis and constipation.[4] Not bad for a safe touch that doesn't cost a dime and can be done anytime, anywhere!

All of this blessing business leads to better sleep and, thus, better mental, emotional and physical health. A good night's sleep washes the brain and body with growth hormones; renews the skin and bones; bolsters the immune system; regenerates the kidneys, lungs and heart; lowers the risk of heart attack, stroke and cancer; regulates hormone levels; and tells our bodies to burn fat away.

If the last thing children carry on their minds before they drift off to sleep is the assurance that they are known, loved, blessed, secure and cared for, their brains are going to fall asleep more easily and solve problems better. (For more information on the problem-solving power of sleep, see the Epilogue, "Why Nighttime Is the Right Time.")

Maxed to the Max

I realize all parenting is a challenge today, but a while back while doing research for my doctoral dissertation, I ran across a couple in Baton Rouge, Louisiana, facing a particularly difficult situation. Unable to have a child of their own, Karen and Louis Decell chose to adopt a baby whose biological father operated a crystal meth lab and whose biological mother was his father's customer during the pregnancy.

After being trained in FAITH5 by their pastor, Fred Wideman at Broadmoor UMC, the Decells tried bits and pieces of the faith practices for a while in their home. When challenges arose, however, they often let it slide. Karen took a second shot at it, however, after a seminar with me. She returned and implemented all five steps with some success. A few weeks later, she sent me the following email. I share it to show how these five nightly enrichuals are helping one brave couple partner with God in some beautiful ways under an extremely challenging circumstance.

If they can do it, then you can do it too.

Dear Rich,

I wanted you to know why FAITH5 is so vital in our household. Since our pastor introduced us to the program, we have been doing a watered-down version of it for a couple of years. Since I do seven-year-old Max's nighttime routine, I was the one who talked to him about highs and lows, read a Scripture, prayed over him and blessed him. My husband, Louis, did the same with Mickey, our youngest son, who is four.

Max is adopted. We got to be in the delivery room when he was born, and we took him home when he was six days old. His birth father had a crystal meth lab. His birth mother was a customer of the lab while they were dating. Thanks to our pediatrician, we know Max has ADHD.

Our pediatrician has also mentioned oppositional defiance disorder. He always says "ODD-ish," because he thinks Max only displays these tendencies occasionally, but his behavior at home more than tests our patience at times. Between the defiance and what I will hereafter refer to as "the genes" (the alcoholism and addiction genes), we are placing Max's future fully in God's hands.

When Max was three, WebMD and I did a self-diagnosis and determined that I had an ulcer. The ulcer turned out to be Mickey. Now Mickey has "the genes" and "the other genes." We don't know if Max and Mickey will choose the straight and narrow path that we are praying for, but one of the things we want to instill in our boys is that they will know deep down how much God loves them. Not just how much God loves everyone, but how much God loves Max and Mickey. They may make some not-so-good choices, but we want them to remember that God still loves them, and we do too.

Max had a huge blow-up a few nights ago. I have to confess that it was your fault. We got in late from a literacy night at Max's school, so our schedule was off. (Max is certainly a kid who needs his routine.) I told the boys they had 20 minutes to hop in and out of a shower and brush their teeth. Any leftover time of that 20 minutes would be spent on a pillow fight. They spent more time playing than showering and brushing their teeth and had no time left for a pillow fight. Well, Max went into a rage over this. Can we blame this on you in any way?

In his rage, Max was yelling stuff at us and attempting to take pillows away from us. He was so angry. He said he didn't want to do FAITH5 and left the room. However, when we started, he sneaked back in with a slightly less defiant attitude and calmed down.

It makes us so sad to see Max act this way, as we are not sure how much of it he can control. However, it means the world to us to be able to bend down over that child, who is not one to show remorse, draw that cross on him and tell him, "You belong to God, to Mommy and Daddy, forever and ever." We add the line you taught us: "Nothing you can say or do will ever make us stop loving you."

While our insides are still churning with all those emotions and it takes us an hour or two to calm down, Max goes off to sleep quickly, blessed in knowing that the God of the universe and his parents love him no matter what. You can see why we need FAITH5 at our house and why we can't imagine raising these two without it.

Karen

In my response to Karen, I told her that the consistent care they were showing Max would eventually rewire and reshape his brain, his heart, his future and the futures of everyone his life touches. The hard truth is that while they could do everything right with Max, they could still lose. He could still break their hearts.[5]

The same is true with your children. There are just too many variables out of your control today. Your children can get in with the wrong friends, make terrible decisions, tell you to go to hell for loving them, and put you through hell for even trying. But the great news is that just because you may think you've failed, you haven't really failed if you've given your heart away in love to a child in need.

In Karen and Louise's case, attempting a great act of love and sacrifice for Max did not represent failure. In fact, attempting such an impossible thing was, in and of itself, a great success. Such an act is the true meaning of noble love. It is the heart of God.

Always remember that you have a God for whom the word "impossible" doesn't exist. You have a Lord Jesus who walked from the grave. You have a Holy Spirit whose power is bigger than your biggest problem. You have a love that will wrestle your children's future from the edge of a ledge to the center of hope.

Love. Give. Pray. Try. Trust. Bless. Then love and bless again. God will work the miracle. That's what God does best.

Blessings from God in early Genesis were all tied to being fruitful and multiplying. Does not the blessing from God today encourage and empower us to be bigger than we are, spreading out to reach and bless more people?

KERRI CLARK

A Theology of Blessing

Blessing is an ancient custom with deep, rich, beautiful, theological roots. God gave the very first blessing in the Bible to Adam and Eve with the charge, "Be fruitful and multiply!" (Gen. 1:28). This first blessing had to do with having babies—and lots of them!

After that, blessings and promises rained down upon Abraham and Sarah's family when God said, "I will bless you and make your name great, so that you will be a blessing!" (Gen. 12:2). Even in the hopeless days of Abraham and Sarah's infertility, they held on to the promised blessing of God with faith, and it paid off in laughter. (Their baby Isaac's name means laughter!)

After that time, more blessings came with promises to Abraham and Sarah's children, and to their children's children. Even in the darkest days of political uncertainty, war and exile, God's promised blessing gave the people hope: "For surely I know the plans I have for you, says the Lord, plans for your welfare and not for harm, to give you a future with hope" (Jer. 29:11). Future. Hope. Good times for God's family one day, if they would only hold on. That is what blessing was in Bible days.

That is also what blessing is today: a promise of God with a future and a hope for you and your family! The hope comes not from an awareness of the present situation; it comes in knowing *who* you are and *whose* you are and *how* God is going to take care of you. The blessing involves placing yourself humbly under the loving care of the living God and holding on to Him in faith.[6]

The Hole, the Holy and the Whole

Blessing flows from God through us, not from things to us. When we give a blessing, we give a gift, but we are not the givers. God is the giver. Blessing shows us that we are partners with God in faith.

When we become the bless-ers, God works in us and with us. God works in, with, under, around and through us to channel divine love and grace into the world. When we become the bless-er, God opens doors for us and for those God blesses through us. It's not us; we are but vessels of the holy wine. We become radio tuners for a message divine. In blessing, God breaks into the world, shakes the world, and remakes the world into the kind of place God wants it to be.

Blessing helps us be the change we seek. It allows us to open ourselves up to the love of God. It enables us to see things in different ways. We become conduits of grace and sacred agents of a holy higher power.

In blessing others, we become sowers of God's seeds. Blessing is a hospital and a hospitality. It changes our image of the other person, of ourselves, and of God. In blessing, we are able to recognize God and bring the will, the power and the presence of God back to mind. Blessing is practical compassion incarnate. When a blessing channels through us, God's power channels to us. When a blessing lands on us, confidence lands on us. The Holy Spirit lands on us, and it soaks in.

Blessing brings new hope and a promise of life. It brings love to flesh and flesh to love. Blessing shows us that our destiny is secured in God. Blessing is refreshing. It brings peace, place and power into the core of our lives. It speaks the positive directly into the negative of a situation and into the core of our very being.

Blessing allows us to see ourselves as part of others, as part of the solutions, and as part of God's bigger purpose and plan. It signifies that something else has entered the moment—that there is something and someone bigger than our problems who can hold us when we aren't able to hold ourselves. God enters our emptiness—the hole—with the holy and holds out hope that the hole in our hearts can be whole again.

Blessings in the Bible

The following are seven blessings from the Bible. Use one each morning and each night this week:

Sunday: The Lord bless you and keep you; the Lord make his face to shine upon you, and be gracious to you; the Lord lift up his countenance upon you, and give you peace (Num. 6:24-26).

Monday: I will make of you a great nation, and I will bless you, and make your name great, so that you will be a blessing (Gen. 12:2).

Tuesday: The Lord will keep you from all evil; he will keep your life. The Lord will keep your going out and your coming in from this time on and forevermore (Ps. 121:7-8).

Wednesday: May God be gracious to us and bless us and make his face to shine upon us, that your way may be known upon earth, your saving power among all nations (Ps. 67:1-2).

Thursday: The grace of the Lord Jesus Christ, the love of God, and the communion of the Holy Spirit be with all of you (2 Cor. 13:13).

Friday: Now may our Lord Jesus Christ himself and God our Father, who loved us and through grace gave us eternal comfort and good hope, comfort your hearts and strengthen them in every good work and word (2 Thess. 2:16-17).

Saturday: Grace, mercy, and peace will be with us from God the Father and from Jesus Christ, the Father's Son, in truth and love (2 John 1:3).

The Bless-er and the Bless-ee

A hug is a blessing. A kiss is a blessing. A smile is a blessing. These all have power. But by invoking (*in+voce*, meaning "in voice") the name of God, we invite Him into the picture with our loved ones, and our loved ones into the picture with God.

When we bless someone, we become ambassadors of the God of the universe. We give a gift from God that is not our own, and as we give it, we are blessed with the honor of giving it and are doubly blessed in the giving. When we receive a blessing, we receive multiple holy gifts . . . a glimpse of eternity . . . a moment with God in the center.

Blessing brings smiles. Blessing names us, claims us and calls us to live up to that name—God's child. It calls us further to live up to this gift. Blessing brings intent and purpose to our lives. It assures, ensures and reassures us of God's unfathomable power and unconditional love.

Blessing brings joy—deep internal joy. This is more than just happiness, which has more to do with the "happenstance" of things around us. Blessing brings joy from deep within us to the surface, connects it to the transcendent, and allows the joy of the Lord to transfer and sink deep to fill the hollows of another human heart.

Isn't That Spatial? (Beam Me Up, Scotty)

When we are blessed, we feel special; but when we give a blessing, we become spatial. Blessing turns a dining room or bedroom into a sacred space. It turns a table or bed into a transport station for the God of the universe to enter our world again and again. Blessing allows us to return, refocus and remember who we are, whose we are, and who we are called to be. It brings Christ into the midst of where two or three are gathered in His name. It calls down the name, the power and the presence of God into flesh. Blessing brings joy, warmth and love. It firms, confirms and reaffirms.

Jacob the Cheating Ankle-Grabber

Blessing changes and rearranges. In some cases, it commutes a death sentence. When the cheating ankle-grabber Jacob (whose name literally meant "the supplanter") latched onto the angel and wrestled, he shouted, "I will not let you go unless you bless me!"

Jacob was fighting for a blessing he did not deserve. He knew he was a cheat. He knew he was a scoundrel. He knew he was in so much trouble and deserved everything his murderous brother was going to rain down upon him the next day. But he held onto the angel and wouldn't let go. "I won't let you go until you bless me!"

Jacob needed the blessing that day. The Angel of the Lord gave it, but he didn't just get Jacob out of his problems. God didn't simply change the situation. God changed Jacob's name from "Ankle-Grabbing Cheat" to "Israel" (meaning "he wrestles/strives with God.")

Blessing doesn't simply change the situation. It changes us. Wow!

The Great Equalizer

Blessing is the great equalizer. A child can bless a parent, just as a parent can bless a child. I've seen two-year-olds reach out of the crib to put a cross on their parents' foreheads. I've seen parents in tears when they raise a child who thinks, *I'm here to bless the world! You got a problem with that?*

When I marked our children with the sign of the cross—the symbol of the greatest love, greatest sacrifice, and greatest story in the history of humanity—it reminded them (and me) of who they were and whose they were. This symbol means more than love itself; it represents and re-presents an undying love that came in dying love. It stood (and still stands) for atonement or, as my mother used to call it, "at-one-ment." In the life, death and resurrection of Jesus Christ, we have become reconciled and "at one" with God.

The cross symbolizes a Jesus who took the whipping, the nails and the insults silently in our place. He went to hell so that we would not have to do so. As a Christian father, I chose to touch my children on the forehead with that amazing mark every night so that the two inches beyond their foreheads—the part of their forebrains that made them human and humane—would be marked with a Jesus hunger forever.

Mark your children as Christ's every night, whether they are awake or asleep. Tell them loudly, clearly and repeatedly that no matter where they go, they belong to Christ. No matter where they go, they have been marked with His brand and His seal. No matter where they go or where they wander—no matter how prodigal they become or what pigs they find themselves lying next to in the mud— they belong to you, to the story, to the sacrifice, and to the God of the greatest love in the universe.

A Little Too . . . Catholic?

My first Baptist friend to embrace FAITH5 and apply it to his own nightly home ritual was Jon Messer, a professor at Virginia Theological Seminary. I called him "Jon the Baptist." Back when Jon was a graduate student, he hosted one of my earliest family ministry seminars. Jon saw the value in all the pieces, but he thought that tracing a cross on his sons' heads was a little too . . . shall we say . . . Catholic?

I told him, "Try it. You'll like it!"

Jon went home from the training event and began doing it as a blessing over his sons. A couple weeks later, I received a note from my secretary that said, "Call Jon immediately." I wondered what the emergency message might be, so I got on the phone right away.

"You're not going to believe this," Jon said. "My five-year-old is going around Dairy Queen putting crosses on people's heads."

A year or so later, I received a second message in the form of an email:

> Rich, I had to write and share this with you. Since Joel was born (he is now two), we have shared highs, lows and blessings each night. For the last few months, Joel has been blessing us by trying to make the sign of the cross and saying, "May the peace of Christ be yours."
>
> Since I am now back in school, I get home late two nights a week, and tonight was one of those nights. I like to give a blessing even if the children are not awake to receive it. Tonight, Joel was drifting off to sleep when I entered. I leaned over to give him a kiss, and he stuck his hand up, pointed with his index finger, and made the sign of the cross on my forehead without my saying or doing anything. He knew what to do and wanted to do it!
>
> I am richly blessed and had to share with you the impact this is having on my family. Joshua is still blessing, and he now must have his blessing from Joel and must bless Joel before going to bed. This is an incredible gift that cannot be described but must be experienced by every child and every parent. Keep up the mission work!
>
> Jon Messer, a Baptist baby blesser

Beautiful!

The Priceless Gifts of Blessing

Blessing is a gift that comes with the power to shape, mold, change and hold the people you love most. It comes with three priceless gifts you can give every morning and every night. These gifts are cheap, because they don't cost you a thing; but also valuable, because they come in the name of God. These gifts will provide your children with assurance and unconditional love every night of their lives. They can forever change your children's futures and the futures of your unborn grandchildren and great-grandchildren.

What are these three costless but priceless gifts?

1. Time
2. Touch
3. Attention

Sometimes all it takes to break a tension is attention.

Just as prayers are powerful "when you lie down and when you rise," a nightly and a morning blessing can set the tone of the day in a positive way and make your child aware of the presence and power of God's guiding hand. A blessing can be as simple as "God bless you! Have a wonderful, funderful, thunderful day!"

God went out and womped us with the water and the Word. We're branded, and now we are (beat) part of the herd. Moo.

MONTY LYSNE

Part II: Broken Hearts and Missing Pieces

When a Child Wanders

In the last chapter, we read a letter from a mother who was heartbroken because the son she raised in Christ had wandered. She regularly wept on his bed in prayer, waiting for him to come to his senses and return to the joy and hope of Christ's love.

What can a Christian parent do when their children leave the loving arms of the Church and abandon everyone who loved them, nurtured them, supported them and made them who they are? What would you say to a parent of children who wander away after they trained them in the way they should go? Who reject the hope that is in them? Who abandon everything the parent stands for, everything the parent knows can give their children a stronger, more beautiful, more meaningful and hopeful life? What can you do? What *should* you do? What if that parent is you?

First, hold fast in prayer. Remember that you are not the Holy Spirit. That job is already filled—and thank God for that!

Second, hold fast to the promises of God. Do you think for one moment God will not be faithful if you have marked your children, named them, claimed them, christened them, dedicated them or baptized them? Will not the Father take care of and protect His own children? Come on—God is faithful! God is going to get them. The Shepherd will not rest until He brings them back. Jesus made it clear that this is the nature and relentless power of our loving God.

Third, recognize that your timing is not God's timing. God will do His work in His way on His time. As much as it would bring you joy if your children came back today, realize this might not happen until they are 24 . . . or 34 . . . or 44. Remember that the promise of Proverbs 22, "bring up a child in the way he should go," ends with "*when he is old* he will not depart from it" (emphasis added). That might not be until they are 64, but you have to believe that God's promises are true. Receive it! Cling to it! Celebrate it! You do your job, and let God do His.

For now, each night that you are blessed to have them under your roof and under your care, look into their eyes. Smile Christ's smile. Mark them, bless them, touch them and brand them with the cross.

This nightly gift and marking will sink deep into their psyches and souls, reminding them they've been marked by love. They belong to God. They are part of the herd. No matter where they go or where they wander, God is going to find them. God is going to get them. God is going to protect them. God is going to bring them back home. Period. If they know Christ and have experienced His loving, healing presence and blessing in your home, they will come back. But if they have no recollection of His loving touch in your gentle hands and gracious heart, then they can't come back.

You can't come back to a place you've never been.

So whatever your situation, and whomever you might have living under your roof, don't let a single night go by without giving the gift of your complete love and attention, sharing highs and lows, turning and returning to the Word, talking about how it might apply to your lives, praying for one another's highs and lows, and offering a physical blessing.

You won't have these children forever. They'll be gone before you know it. In a very real sense, all parenting is an intentional interim ministry. So, ministers, do your duty! Tend the flock of God that is in your charge. Get the issues of the day out in the open. Get real, deal and heal, and then end each day with a loving, inclusive blessing.

Mark your children with a kiss and a cross. Let them know every night as you hold and enfold them in your arms just how precious they are to you and to God. Let them hear again and again who they are and whose they are. Bless and release, and let God do the rest. You can count on God's power and love to bring them back. I sure do.

What Happens to a Child Who Isn't Blessed?

How important is a blessing to a child? Pastor Keith Andrew Spencer once shared a sad story about a woman who called late one night, crying on the phone. The woman's mother had just experienced a stroke and was dying. "I still don't know if . . . if she ever loved me!" the sobbing woman said. "Now I'll never know."

The woman who called was Andrew's mother. She was 68. Grandma died, and his mother never knew if she had ever been loved or not. This is what happens to a child who isn't blessed. Perhaps a line from Simon and Garfunkel's "I Am a Rock" captures it best: "Hiding in my room, sealed within my tomb, I touch no one and no one touches me. I am a rock, I am an island, and a rock feels no pain and an island never cries."[7]

A rock feels no pain? An island never cries? Maybe not until it takes so much heat that it shatters and explodes. Then everyone cries.

The Daddy Blessing Void

Perhaps the best way to understand what happens when parents fail to bless their children can be seen in what I call "the Daddy Void," which could just as easily be called the "Daddy Blessing Void." In my opinion, we don't have a teenage violence problem in this country—we have an absent father problem. Just consider some of the data.

Of the top 50 serial killers in the last 100 years, 49 were male, and those males accounted for between 1,631 (proven) and 2,581 (estimated) murders.[8] In the last 30 years, there have been 62 school shootings in the United States, and 61 of those 62 shooters were male.[9] A few years back, the FBI did a study of 17 school shooters and only found two things in common: all were boys, and nearly all had a father problem. As NFL pro Bill Glass states, "There's something about it when a man doesn't get along with his father. It makes him mean; it makes him dangerous; it makes him angry."

Newton, Connecticut. Aurora, Colorado. Columbine, Colorado. Virginia Tech, Virginia. While genetics might have been the culprit in some of these cases, I am haunted by the question as to how many of these young men would have turned out differently if they had been raised with a father who opened up his heart every night, asked them to share their highs and lows, and closed each day by laying his hands on them with loving words and a gentle blessing. As author Frank Hammond writes:

> The benefits of the father's blessing are far-reaching and readily make the difference between success and failure; victory and defeat; happiness and misery in an individual's life. The absence of the blessing makes way for the curse to lay hold.[10]

Sadly, even when a father is physically present in our homes today, he is often emotionally absent from the nightly care routine. Our families, our nation and our world need men to both grow up and show up. We need fathers to get out of the stands, get into the game, and step up to the plate. We need women who are strong enough to settle for nothing less in a man than a true father who is there physically, emotionally and spiritually for their children.

An emotionally abusive father may be worse than no father at all, but a father who abandons his children every night while in the same house may do far more damage than one who walks out the door and never returns. Either way, we have a father problem. Either way, we have a systemic disease in our society that we must attack, or it will continue to attack us. Either way, we need a father solution.

Invisible Sailing Ships

I recall an old college professor teaching about the Native Americans who first saw the huge European sailing ships. They didn't know what they were seeing. Because of their lack of exposure—their lack of a frame of reference—the ships were virtually invisible to them. They didn't see the ships because they had never seen them before. They only saw strange clouds.

There's a strange paradox on the nature of sight. When it comes to your eyes, you can't see what you haven't seen. Because the Native Americans had never before seen ships, they couldn't see them when they were right off the coast. Neurologically, sight isn't really sight. It's an array of photons hitting the retina, bouncing to the optic nerve, and flying past the linguistic/phonic centers in the prefrontal cortex. Because of this, the static firings of a billion wirings must be interpreted in multiple areas of the brain all along the way. This array of firings and wirings can only be interpreted through the lens of what the brain has already seen and already knows. If the brain hasn't seen the pattern before, it doesn't know what it is looking at.

The human brain can't build anything unless it has the building blocks already in place. Taking this one step further, you can't learn what you don't already know. You can't see what you haven't already seen. You can't be what you haven't seen someone else be. You can't become anything unless someone has gone before you to show you the way. The what. The how. The who.

You need a frame of reference. A frame of reverence.

You Can't Be What You Can't See

This is why a boy who grows up with zero exposure to a strong, loving, wise and healthy male role model will have a nearly impossible time learning how to become one. When he enters adolescence, the testosterone flood that comes with it may push him away from his mother and lead to him being raised by the media, videogames and peers. He might as well be raised by a pack of wolves.

One of the first laws of physics is that a vacuum will always be filled. The boy will look for a father figure in a teacher, a coach, a youth worker or a gang leader on the streets. But that surrogate father will never be what a daddy could have been. That person will never fill the psychological, sociological and neurological void that someone who tucks him in every night will fill.

That boy will grow up never knowing exactly what he missed but vaguely aware that he wasn't worth enough to be known, to be "friended," or to be loved. He will never know the feeling of being led and guided by an emotionally available man who would literally lay down his life for his beloved son. He won't know what a real daddy is, nor will he know how to become one. If a boy doesn't see it, he can never be it.

Likewise, a girl growing up without a loving, encouraging, protecting father will seek to fill that void in any way she can. Ninety percent of women and children in prostitution were abused—not nurtured, cherished and protected—by the males in their lives. According to Dr. Paul Dobransky:

> Fathers teach their daughters about men, both through their stories, and through personal example—being the very first man she has ever encountered and "fallen in love with." Fathers show their daughters they are valuable and precious, and will always, always be protected and safe, but that they have guts and strength and resolve no less than a man. If he can see to it, he will always be there for you to help, to remind you of who you are when you are confused or stressed, and that you are not just any girl or woman, a statistic in today's confusing social and romantic arenas, or a cog in a corporate wheel, but his daughter.[11]

The (Virtually) Single Mother

I know that what I have shared above about the Daddy Void is a harsh truth, because there are so many wonderful, caring and sacrificial single mothers out there who are doing their best to raise sons and daughters with zero emotional or financial support from the father. I also know there are millions of marvelous and exhausted married moms out there who are, by default, taking responsibility for 100 percent of the spiritual lives of their children. The male figure may be providing physically and financially, but he has not made a deposit into his children's spiritual bank in years (if ever). For all practical purposes, these brave and caring moms are serving as spiritual single parents.

However, the more I study the neurology of infant, toddler and teen development, the more I have come to believe two politically incorrect conclusions. I know I'll take some heat for this because of the present mood and cultural climate that often considers men irrelevant in the raising of children. I am sorry if it hurts, but here goes.

Politically Incorrect Conclusion #1

Single moms, here's my difficult advice for you. I believe there is no substitute for a healthy, loving, encouraging and emotionally available daddy who is there for his children. Psychologically, sociologically, financially and neurologically speaking, there is no substitute for a father who believes in his children, cheers for his children, dreams with his children, and schemes with his children. There is no substitute for a daddy who blesses his children, takes the wild and sometimes rocky ride of adolescence with his children, and gives his children the consistent message that they are terrific. Agree or disagree if you wish, but here are the statistics.

- 90 percent of runaways are fatherless.
- 90 percent of repeat arsonists are fatherless.
- 85 percent of all youth in prison are fatherless.
- 85 percent of those who exhibit behavioral disorders come from fatherless homes.

- 80 percent of rapists motivated with displaced anger lack a father.
- 75 percent of adolescent patients in chemical abuse centers are fatherless.
- 71 percent of pregnant teenagers lack a father.
- 70 percent of juveniles in state-operated institutions lack a father.

Statistics also show that preschoolers who do not live with both biological parents are 40 times more likely to be sexually abused.[12] A child without a father is 32 times more likely to end up homeless and on the streets; 20 times more likely to exhibit behavior disorders; 14 times more likely to become a rapist; and 5 times more likely to commit suicide.[13]

Single moms, no matter how hard you try, you cannot fill this emotional void alone. If there is no healthy male in your child's life right now, get to your church, get to your family, or get to the local boys' club and call out a grandpa or surrogate uncle to commit to regularly sharing highs, lows, prayers and blessings with your children. Do it in person, via Skype or on the phone, but start tonight. Then do it every night! There is simply too much at stake for your precious children's futures.

For those moms who have a man in the house who isn't lifting his share of the spiritual weight, your message to him tonight—and every night from this day forth—needs to be crystal clear: "If you're not tucking my babies in bed, you're not getting in bed with me either."

Politically Incorrect Conclusion #2

Single dads, here's my difficult advice for you. I am convinced from a neurological standpoint that not only do children need a healthy father figure, but that they also need a healthy, loving, touching, singing mother. Children need a mother for cuddles, comfort, confidence and care when they are small. There is no biological, hormonal or immunological replacement for the hugs, kisses, comfort, laughter and even the scoldings that come from a mother.

From the very start, a mother imprints love, life and health to her children. Because a baby's ears are fully operational (myelinated) in the womb, that baby is born already knowing and preferring his or her mother's voice and knowing his or her mother's songs. A surrogate mother will always be playing catch-up with both bonding and baby brain development. It can be done, but she will have to work overtime in the early years to compensate for not being the birth mother.

For a girl to turn into a healthy, secure woman (and a healthy mother herself one day), she needs to know a mother. She needs to grow up with one. It will be nearly impossible for her to play that role herself one day if she has received no role model. As Queen Elizabeth once responded when asked how she learned to be queen, "I learned the same way monkeys do—I watched my mother." Likewise, for a boy to turn into a healthy man who respects, loves and cherishes women, he needs a healthy mother for his brain development and a nurturing and respectful father for his social and emotional development.

So, for you single dads, if your child does not have a steady, consistent, healthy, loving mother figure in his world, you need to find one to serve in a surrogate capacity. Get to your church. Get to your family. Get to your neighbors and beg, con, bribe and cajole a healthy, strong woman to embrace your children in that role. It's just too important not to have one. A child without a mother or a completely committed and available surrogate mother figure will grow up with poverty in her neurons and a hole in her soul. You can't fill this role.

Loving to Know and Knowing to Love

Now that I've made these two statements, let me back up for a moment and explain the science behind these conclusions. In her book *Loving to Know*, Esther Meek writes, "Rather than knowing in order to love, we love in order to know." There's another beautiful line that struck me: "We are born into someone's arms."[14]

I recall a professor back in college saying that we are born believing that the world is simply an extension of ourselves. The universe revolves around us. It isn't until later in our development that we come to see others as others, as individuals other than ourselves. This makes me wonder about our fundamental attitude toward life, love and existence. When we enter the world, will we perceive our universe to be a welcoming place or a hostile one? Will it be one in which our basic needs will be met? Will it be a place where we will be loved? Where we will be safe?

As our neurons begin to focus and comprehend, a healthy mother *and* father will emerge from this fog as the answer to all of our immediate and essential questions. Mother is the first "other" we will experience, as she represents a connection with our inner selves. To us, she is life. She is sustenance. She is safety. She is touch. She is food. She is love.

As we grow, we begin to develop a will and self of our own within our mother's gaze and embrace. Our father joins as we take our first steps, say our first words, make our first falls and do our first everything. Our parents' applause guides us and goads us on. We are born into someone's arms, and those arms surround us, shape us and shield us. They fundamentally represent the folding and scaffolding that enable us to become the person who emerges. Without the presence of these healthy parents in our lives, there will be no healthy "us." It is as simple and as complex as that.

There is a reason God made us male and female. There is a reason the two become one when a baby is born (see Gen. 2:24). This isn't so much about sex as it is about life. A child needs a mother and a father. So, again, if your children don't have these types of role models in their lives, for their sakes go and find one. You owe it to them. You owe it to you. You made this child, and now the child can make you. God gave you this gift. Now gift this child with their best chance.

Part III: The Day I Died

Gone in a Heartbeat

Throughout this book I have stressed several reasons why I believe you need to begin *now* to take these steps to build a healthier family.

As we close out this chapter, I want to give you another one: You will not be around forever, and you never know when your time will be up. If you miss this chance to bless your children now, you may never have the opportunity to give them this gift for their lives.

I know firsthand just how fragile life can be, because while some people carry a rock or a cross around in their pocket, I carry nitroglycerin. Good stuff. It started when I was 52 and I started feeling some pressure in my chest. I had been under a lot of stress both at home and at work, so I thought I had better check it out.

I knew I had a history of heart disease in my family. My grandpa (my mom's dad) died on my mom's wedding day at the age of 52. My mom, Kathryn Marie, experienced two heart attacks before she died. Her brother, Jim, and sister, Wanda, both had heart attacks when they were young. I knew I shouldn't mess with genetics, so I went into the local clinic for a set of tests. The doctors finished their procedures, looked at the charts, and said, "Inconclusive. Come back in two weeks."

I went home every night for two weeks and felt more and more pressure. Two weeks later, I showed up at the hospital. The doctors filled my veins with radioactive dye and set me on a treadmill, and then put me into a huge machine to look at me in 3D. They studied the tests and said, "Inconclusive. Come back in two weeks."

I thought, *I'm going to be dead in two weeks! I'm going to the cardiac specialty hospital in St. Paul.* So I made an appointment. The first time they could see me was . . . in two weeks!

The Goodbye Letter

When I arrived at the cardiac hospital, the doctors said, "Here's what we're going to do. We're going to stick a needle up through your groin, wind it all the way into your heart, and fill it full of dye. If we find any problems, we will balloon up the blockage and install a little wire stent in the spot. There's no problem with this. We do it all the time. By the way, we only have complications with 1 out of 100,000 people."

This did not comfort me in the least, because my mother had always told me I was one in a million. So the doctors finished the exam and told me to come back in . . . two weeks! On the night before I was to go in for the procedures, I had to sign a pile of releases. The last form required me to promise not to sue the hospital if I died. I thought, *Oh, buddy, if I die I'm coming for you!*

That night I couldn't sleep. I lay tossing and turning until 3 AM. The pressure was building, so I got up, went to my computer, and cleared the entire cluttered screen of everything except three files: (1) a goodbye letter to my kids, (2) a final blessing, and (3) a quickly recorded song. I thought, *If anything happens, at least I will have those files waiting for my babies.*

My note told my children how proud I was of them and how much joy they had given me. The blessing was a combination of "I'm happy to be your pappy," "Daddy will always love you no matter what; Mommy will always love you no matter what; Jesus will always love you no . . . matter . . . what," and "there's nothing you can ever say and nothing you can ever do that will ever stop God's awesome heart from always loving you."

The song I recorded was a little tune I had written for my kids back when they were babies—a song I would sing in the hallway as a final blessing after I had turned out the lights and left their rooms. It went like this:

Who do you think loves you?
Who do you think cares?
Who do you think loves to see you
At the top of the stairs when he comes home?

[Turning toward Kathyrn's door]
Who do you think will miss you
When you step into the world?
Who do you think will always think of you
As Daddy's little girl?

[Turning toward Joseph's door]
Who do you think will miss you
When you come to say goodbye?
Who do you think will always think of you
As Daddy's little guy?

[Bridge]
And when I'm much too old to hold you on my knee
I'll thank the Lord above that you will always be
My ba-ya-ya-be!

Who do you think loves you?
Who do you think cares?
Who do you think loves to see you
At the top of the stairs when he comes home?
Who do you think will miss you
When you step into the world and say goodbye
Who do you think will always think of you
As Daddy's girl and guy!

I left the note, blessing and song on top of my screen saver and, finally feeling some peace, went to sleep for three hours.

The Surgery

I arrived at the St. Paul Cardiac Center at 6 AM. The doctors and nurses did the prep, took me into the operating room, opened me up, and found 80 percent blockage in the coronary artery that goes around the back of my heart. They inserted a balloon, opened the artery, and set a stent in place. They found 60 percent blockage in the right side of my heart, but didn't put a stent in (they don't do that until the blockage is at least 70 percent). My numbers started jumping all over the place, so they said, "Let's just pull this plug now and stop."

I woke in recovery with Arlyce holding my hand. "The doctor was just here," she said. "Good thing we caught it. You could've been dead before you hit the parking lot. And no more cheeseburgers."

No more cheeseburgers? I thought. Did I want to live if there were no more cheeseburgers? "Okay, okay," I said. "No more cheeseburgers."

"By the way," she added, "the doctor said three things have to change: diet, exercise and stress."

"Get him back in here. I'm going for two out of three."

Arlyce and I sat together awhile. I was still groggy under medication. Then I remembered that our beautiful daughter had just had her wisdom teeth pulled the day before. She was probably sitting home alone and was miserable. "Go home," I said. "Be with Kathryn. I'll be fine. I'm not going anywhere. Go home."

Flat-lining

Within a few minutes of Arlyce's leaving, the world turned yellow and the room began to spin. I started getting dizzy, but I thought it was just the medication. When the nurse came in, her eyes lit up. "Oh . . . we've got an embolism the size of a golf ball here. Let's take care of that." She applied pressure and, trained in diversion tactics, asked, "What do you do for a living?"

"I help parents survive adolescence." That was all I could think of saying.

"Funny," she smiled. "I have a 13-year-old who won't talk to me."

"Sweetheart!" I said. "You can hurt him financially! You just tell him if he doesn't have five minutes for his mama, you won't have five cents for his car insurance when he turns 16!" As I proceeded to tell her about how to do FAITH5, I started to feel really strange. Like floating-out-of-your-body strange.

"I'm feeling really odd here," I said.

"Let's turn you on your side—"

That was the last thing I heard before my heart stopped.

"Beeeeeeee . . ." The EKG machine screamed. "Beeeeeeeeeeee . . ." Then I heard nothing. I was gone.

They tell me that the doctors pounded on me awhile and stuck a needle in my heart the size of New Jersey. The next thing I heard was a voice saying, "Welcome back."

"Was I gone?" I asked.

"Oh, yeah, you were gone." A dead Lutheran. Bet you never met one of those before.

You don't want to make the wrong mistake.
YOGI BERRA

Second Chances

Looking back on my life since that fateful day, I can truly say that my death was the best thing that ever happened to me. (Not everyone can say that.) I had a near-death experience. I do not intend to let the rest of my years be a near-life experience.

I came out of the ICU with a much better sense of what matters (God, my wife, my children), what doesn't matter (most of what used to matter), and what to worry about (not much). After all, I've been dead. What more can they do to me? I also have a keener sense of how short time is, how valuable friends are, and how wasting even a single moment is a terrible mistake. The brilliant football coach Lou Holtz once said, "Killing time isn't murder. It's suicide."

I know parents want to give the best to their children. They really do care about their children's physical, mental and emotional needs. But the fact is that most parents put more brain power, intent and strategizing into planning a weekend road trip than they do in designing and planning their children's spiritual journey. Most parents who dedicated their children to God long ago haven't dedicated a single night in their home to God ever since. Even good church folks are often more comfortable hiring a good youth worker or other spiritual mercenary to care for their children's spiritual needs than stepping up and taking on that responsibility themselves.

Here's the reality: The job of parenting cannot be hired out. The best cannot happen without you. You are the most invested. You have the most at stake. And whether you know it or not (or choose to believe it or not), you are the best qualified. God gave this child to you, and no one loves them as you do. No one can help them like you can. No one has access to them when they're getting ready to sleep—the most meaning-filled moments of the day.

It's time you make a personal, intentional and consistent commitment to invest in your children's spiritual needs. What's the investment? Don't take out your wallet or credit card—your money can't buy you the return you seek. Take out your calendar. The only investments that will work are your most valuable currency: time and attention. It is time to invest your most valuable currencies in the most precious and sacred calling God will ever give you: your children.

Most of us don't get a second chance on life or on parenting. But you do. This is why tonight is the most important night of the rest of your life. You can always make more money, but you will never get another tonight. You will never make more time. Time is your only non-renewable currency.

It's not that difficult. You simply need to commit a few minutes. A time. A place. A sacred space. The people you love. A simple plan. A commitment to share, read, talk, pray and bless your family every night of your life as long as you have it in your power. You can give immeasurable psychological, sociological, neurological and theological gifts to your children tonight without spending a nickel. You can give these gifts to the great grandchildren you'll never know. If you only start tonight.

While you're at it, why not write your family a last love letter—a final blessing? Tell them how proud you are of them. Tell them how much you love them. Tell them that you know they will bless the world in wonderful ways and if there's any way God will grant you the gift, you'll be watching them and cheering them on with the great cloud of witnesses. Tell them you can't wait to see them in heaven. Tell them you're sorry if it needs to be said. Tell them you forgive them if it needs to be read. Tell them everything you'd want them to hear as they walk away from your grave.

Place the note somewhere they are sure to find it on that last day. You will never be sorry you did. I know that the next time I die, I want my kids to walk away from my grave taking the best of me and burying the rest of me. Make your final words a blessing, and part of you will walk away from your own grave that day.

The best part.

Death ends a life, not a relationship.
MITCH ALBOM, *TUESDAYS WITH MORRIE*

Blessing from the Grave

I didn't dream about my dad for the first five months after his death. Then a strange gift was given to me one night. After writing this final chapter on blessing and falling to sleep with my laptop on my chest, I had a visitor.

In the dream, I was sitting in a skyscraper conference room finishing a meeting with some executives I didn't recognize. They all rose to leave, and one by one the room emptied. I was standing alone next to a wall of floor-to-ceiling windows on the brightest of bright days. The light was warm and inviting. The skies were radiant, blue and cloudless. Then I felt the presence of someone behind me. I turned. It was dad.

Not the worn, tired, confused shell of the man I had videotaped on the Fourth of July fish picnic. He was fit. Trim. Maybe sixty-fiveish. I noticed that his face was barely wrinkled as he flashed a huge, proud smile. His eyes twinkled with deep joy.

Without a word he stepped up behind me, put his arms around me, and squeezed with a strength I hadn't felt since I was a teenager. Dad didn't say a word. He didn't have to.

I knew I was loved. I knew I was blessed.

I *know* I am blessed.

Thanks for stopping by, Dad. Do come again.

Home Huddle: How to Start

After a little exercise and physical fun to pump oxygen, glucose and BDNF in your child's brain . . .

1. Designate a special place to meet together. Remove all tech and other distractions.
2. Share your highs and lows. Repeat whatever the child says as his or her highs and lows to make sure you heard them right.
3. Read a key verse or story from God's Word.
4. Pause and ask, "What is God trying to say to us tonight with these words?" or "How does this verse connect to our highs and lows tonight?"

5. Pray for one another's highs and lows by name, thanking God for the highs and asking for help with the lows.
6. Bless one another.

There are a few ways to bless your children. One is the "blessing touch," where you give your child a kiss, a hug, or kiss your little finger and mark his or her forehead with the sign of the cross.

Another option is to choose words that show that the blessing is from God. This could be as simple as, "God bless you, I love you, goodnight" or "Jesus loves you, and so do I" or "[Name], child of God, you have been sealed by the Holy Spirit and marked with the cross of Christ forever!" I often used the words, "There is nothing you can ever say and nothing you can ever do that will ever stop God's awesome heart from always loving you."

You might also choose the words of Aaron's blessing (see Num. 6:24-26 below). You could even use a traditional Gaelic blessing: "May the road rise up to meet you. May the wind be always at your back. May the sun shine warm upon your face; the rains fall soft upon your fields and until we meet again, may God hold you in the palm of His hand."

Of course, there's always the "Happy to Be Your Pappy" chant (see the introduction)!

Dream Team Reflections

The Lord bless you and keep you; the Lord make his face to shine upon you, and be gracious to you; the Lord lift up his countenance upon you, and give you peace.
NUMBERS 6:24-26

Gather with your family, friends or a small group of people you trust and respect to share the following.

To watch videos on this theme, learn **Numbers 6:24-26** in song and American Sign Language, and download free weekly devotional resources, go to www.faith5.org/bless.

Dr. Rich Melheim

Reflection 1

Read and highlight the theme verse together in your Bibles. Listen to it in song using the link below. Then ask, "What happens to people when they . . ."

- Receive a blessing from someone they love just before bedtime?
- Give a blessing to someone they love just before bedtime?
- Receive *and* give blessings nearly every night of their young lives, surrounded by people they love?

Reflection 2

Discuss the following together:

- What would giving your children a kiss, a hug, a cross traced across their foreheads, an "I love you" and a "God bless you" every night do for them?
- How would those gifts change them?
- What would those gifts do to your children's sleep and dreams?
- How might it change their relationship with the bless-er?
- How might it change their entry into and exit from adolescence?
- How might it affect their own parenting one day?

Reflection 3

Take a look at the definition of the word "countenance" from dictionary.com:

coun·te·nance: noun. 1. Appearance, esp. the look or expression of the face 2. The face; visage 3. Calm facial expression; composure 4. Approval or favor; encouragement; moral support

How does this definition enrich your understanding of Numbers 6:24?

This Week's Challenge

Commit to doing all five steps of the FAITH5 together each night this week. Take turns sharing highs and lows. Read this week's theme verse and talk about how the Scripture might relate to your highs and lows. Pray in thanks for the highs and ask God's help with the lows. Pull out a newspaper or magazine and find something outside your walls to add to your prayers. Bless one another with a hug, a marked cross, or another safe touch and the words from Numbers 6:24-26: "[Name], the Lord bless you and keep you . . ." Use the free *Bless Home Huddle Journal* download at www.faith5.org/bless/weekly to record your highs, lows and prayers of the week. If you are living alone, commit to calling a parent, family member or friend every night this week to share all five steps. In addition, consider:

- Watching me discuss the power of blessing at www.faith5. org/bless/rich
- Watching *Pastor Ray's Last Days* at www.faith5.org/bless/story
- Learning this week's Bible verse, Numbers 6:24-26, in song and American Sign Language with Christy Smith at www. faith5.org/bless/song

You can also download weekly resources, nightly Bible verses, videos, games and other free resources at www.faith5.org/bless/weekly.

Two Final Challenges

Write a final love letter to your loved ones telling them how honored and blessed you are to be in their lives and how much you love them. Seal the letter with a blessing and a kiss. Make a second copy.

Wondering what these faith practices might look like in real life? Imagine six little boys sitting patiently and obediently on a bedroom floor with their parents. Imagine them taking turns sharing highs and lows, singing Sunday's Scripture verse, talking about how the Scripture relates to their lives, holding hands in prayer and blessing one another. Then check out www.faith5.org/extras.

Place the original letter under their pillow or in the mail. Place the second copy in a strongbox with your will and final papers and instruct your executor to read it the night of your wake or funeral service. With that done, commit to sharing the blessing words and touch along with the rest of FAITH5 for the next 40 days. (Just long enough to build a habit!)

Why Nighttime Is the Right Time

So teach us to count our days that we may gain a wise heart.
PSALM 90:12

My friends David Anderson and Paul Hill at Vibrant Faith Ministries teach the following four keys for practicing faith in a family:

1. Caring conversations
2. Devotions
3. Service
4. Rituals and traditions[1]

If you want to raise a healthy, resilient and faithful child into a healthy, resilient faithful adult, David and Paul's research shows that you need to be intentional about installing these faith practices in the home.

The brilliant John Roberto, president of Lifelong Faith Associates, has carried out multiple studies in support of the same premise.[2] His research shows that family faith practices lower divorce rates, raise marital and family satisfaction, reduce family violence, increase responsible fathering, and reduce risky behaviors in adolescence. John, Paul, David and a host of family experts agree that sharing caring conversations and faith talk at any time during the day is a "net plus" for a family.

To learn **Psalm 90:12** in song and American Sign Language, go to www.faith5.org/extras.

After school, around the dinner table or in the car can all serve as convenient conversation moments for your family. However, in this final section, I will explain why FAITH5 is clearly most effective when done in the last few minutes before your children go to sleep at night. The reason has to do with the maximum problem-solving abilities and deeper meaning-making processes that take place in the human brain during rapid eye movement and slow wave sleep.

As you read this section, I think you will agree that any time is better than no time when it comes to sharing your cares and concerns in a family, but nighttime is the right time for sharing highs and lows, reading Scripture, talking about how the highs and lows might relate to the Scripture, praying and blessing your children.

The hand that rocks the cradle is the hand that rules the world.

WILLIAM ROSS WALLACE

The Psychology of Nighttime Rituals

Psychologically speaking, having consistent and predictable bedtime rituals in place is healthy and comforting for children, as it gives them a greater sense of stability, predictability and control. When children experience the consistency of a caring nightly ritual along with the knowledge that someone else knows what they are going through, it can help their brains resolve issues and set the stage for better sleep.

Children (and adults) who don't get enough sleep tend to focus on and remember the negatives in the day more than the positive. Lack of proper sleep can make a person irritable, jumpy and tense. According to Dr. David Agus of the University of Southern California, the side effects of poor sleep include hypertension, confusion, memory loss, an inability to learn new things, obesity, cardiovascular disease and depression.[3]

In a recent study in the *Journal of Pediatrics,* researchers found that 40 percent of four-year-olds and 60 percent of seven-year-olds had greater difficulties than their non-sleep-deprived counterparts. The study also found that 25 to 50 percent of children and adolescents with sleep problems had attention deficit hyperactivity disorder.[4] Boys who continue with sleep disorders into adulthood are twice as likely to have clinical depression, while girls with sleep problems experience depression at five times the normal rate. Treating sleep disorders early and setting healthy patterns in place before the upheaval of puberty can dramatically improve these psychiatric symptoms in adults.

When children end the day with caring conversation, prayer and blessing—as opposed to sharing these things at mealtime and spending the next few hours with television, texting and homework—it allows the last messages their brains receive prior to drifting off to be positive. Here is where the psychology of nighttime blessing blurs into the neurology. Sharing, caring, massaging, laughing, singing and blessing all allow the brain to sop up cortisol from the bloodstream. This is essential because cortisol, the stress hormone, kills baby nerve cells as they are born and instructs the body to hold on to all the fat it can. In turn, this allows melatonin—the sleep drug—to do its duty.

Thus, FAITH5 before bed is both a brain-enhancer and weight-loss technique. Who woulda thunk it! More on that in a moment.

The Sociology of Nighttime Rituals

Those of you who have laughed, giggled, rocked, prayed, sung, played and whispered a baby to sleep don't need any outside evidence of the bonding power of sharing those last few drowsy minutes of the day. They are magic, meaningful, priceless, exhausting and irreplaceable.

You can't buy those moments. They appear and disappear for such a brief span in the scheme of life. Here to savor, then gone forever. If you are blessed with grandchildren, you may get a second shot at them, but they will also come and go all too fast. They don't last, but traces of them do.

Your children will forget all those moments in their conscious minds. Yet the love you share, the kisses and hugs you give, the stories you tell, and the blessings, prayers and crosses you trace across each sleeping face will lay the neural network for your children to grow into secure adults who can take the world by storm and take the storms in stride. The future you write every night will bless them to their graves. So don't let a night go by without giving and receiving such a blessing.

Sociologically speaking, rituals are important for expressing, fixing and reinforcing shared values and beliefs. We are drawn to trust and appreciate those who share in the ritual and give us the gifts of their time and attention. Returning to, reflecting upon and restating the challenges of the day within the context of a safe and loving family or a family of friends bond us to those people. As Linda Ashford, Ph.D., an assistant professor of pediatrics and psychology at Monroe Carell Jr. Children's Hospital at Vanderbilt, states:

> It is so important to read or tell stories to children at bedtime because in this simple bedtime routine, parents have a chance to create a special world with their children. This shared literary world of childhood is the stuff of dreams, imagination and fantasy; a world from which children launch their own imaginative play and their own stories. In addition, children's literature and shared stories provide a unique opportunity for parent-child intimacy and bonding, a time for closeness and trust-building that prepares the child for the regular, brief but challenging separation that nighttime creates. Children who snuggle close to their parents while being read a story end their day positively, feeling the love and security that every child deserves.[5]

The Neurology of Nighttime Rituals

The strongest argument for having FAITH5 at bedtime—as opposed to dinner or drive time—has to do with how the last few minutes of each day set the stage for a night filled with neural networking, researching, creative problem-solving and solutions. With recent advances in technology, scientists can now see what happens in sleeping brains. They have determined that the areas controlling logic, expectations and socially acceptable restraints are shut down during sleep, while the areas associated with visual images, emotion and perception of movement kick into high gear.

With the senses, censors and logical areas turned off and the visual and emotional areas turned on, anything goes! We can fly over any wall. We can slay any dragon. We can solve any problem. The human brain's brilliance comes from its ability to allow seemingly random and unrelated ideas to collide with other random, unrelated ideas and thoughts (see step 3), and it is in this caldron of the adjacent possible where brilliant dreams are born. Sleep is not merely the bedchamber of transient dreams but also the neural crucible of creative innovation.

Searching the File Cabinets

Given this, researchers now know that the *optimal* time for our brains to work on difficult problems is not during the working day, the classroom day, or even the waking hours, but during sleep! Our brains don't go dormant when we doze off. Rather, they kick into maximum creative meaning-making mode. The answers to life's most vexing problems are actually best incubated, nurtured, taught and caught when our eyes are closed and we are deep and soundly asleep. According to molecular biologist Dr. John Medina, the reason we need sleep is not to turn off the brain but to turn on the brain's learning power:

> If you ever get a chance to listen in on a living brain while it is slumbering, you'll have to get over your disbelief. The brain does not appear to be asleep at all. Rather, it is almost unbelievably active during "rest," with legions of neurons crackling electrical commands to one another in constantly shifting patterns—displaying greater rhythmical activity during sleep, actually, than when it is wide awake.[6]

It appears that the sleeping brain shuts off outward stimuli in favor of inward stimuli and begins a concentrated hunt through the "file cabinets" of what we already know and have in storage. It searches for connections, associations and creative answers to any new challenges the day threw our way.

Cycles in the "Sleeping" Brain

In the 1950s, scientists at the University of Chicago discovered that human sleep consisted of several approximately 90-minute cycles. Each of these cycles contained at least one period of heightened brain activity, which they labeled "rapid eye movement" or REM sleep. REM sleep, when dreaming is most likely, is followed by three other stages, including a slow "non-REM" sleep wave where the brain tries to make sense of the new information, emotions and impressions encountered during the day.

During REM sleep, the brain replays key events of our day thousands of times—often in symbolic and representational ways. (For Christians, this is often where we see God's messages coming through to us.) For instance, we might see a problem as a monster or a rock we can't lift, or we might see a situation in which we feel trapped as a pool of glue that sticks our legs to the ground so that we can't run away.

It is estimated that a waking brain is only consciously aware of 1/10,000 of all the stimuli received during the day. All those images, sounds, smells and other sensory barrages flash past us so quickly that our brain must use its gatekeepers to block out the "noise" so that we can focus and function. If we didn't have those filters, every noise bombarding us at 10,000 bits per second and every image hitting our eyes at 7 billion bits per second would flood and overwhelm our brains. The noise would render us unable to cope with anything. We wouldn't have ADD or ADHD; we'd have ADDDHDDHDDDH.

A Thousand Reruns

During REM sleep, the brain takes important information—that which was important enough to register but remain unnoticed—and re-fires and rewires it thousands of times in an attempt to make sense of it. Then, during the slow non-REM sleep wave, the brain takes those most memorable outward bits of new information—those things that connected with something that was already meaningful to us—and sifts them through the labyrinth of stored memories. In this way, the brain searches for associated connections, combinations of potential solutions, and meaning. It takes the "new" and connects it to the "knew" to make it the most helpful for us.

It's as if the waking brain says, "Here's the new problem, opportunity or challenge, but I can't make sense of it right now. TMI! So I'm going to set it on the desktop tonight and, while I'm asleep, I'm going to assign my staff to search and re-search all the old file cabinets to see if there's something that will help me figure this new thing out." As Dr. Sara Mednick, assistant professor of psychiatry at UC San Diego, states:

> For creative problems you've already been working on, the passage of time is enough to find solutions. However, for new problems, only REM sleep enhances creativity. REM sleep helps achieve such solutions by stimulating associative networks (i.e., looking around for connections to what you already know), and by allowing the brain to make new and useful associations between unrelated ideas.[7]

In other words, our conscious minds are great for working on old problems, but for new solutions to new problems, the subconscious mind is better equipped to go searching through unrelated file cabinets. When our senses are shut down and the gatekeepers and logic centers of our brain are on break, our subconscious mind is free to seek out and find creative solutions to problems the conscious mind wouldn't even consider.

· ·

God speaks in one way, and in two, though people do not perceive it. In a dream, in a vision of the night, when deep sleep falls on mortals, while they slumber on their beds, then he opens their ears.

JOB 33:14-16

· ·

A Theology of Nighttime Rituals

Given that God can speak during waking hours, is it not possible that He can also speak during sleep? The Bible says yes! As the stories of Joseph and Daniel show, God can and does speak through dreams. We just need to have our ears on.

History is filled with people who received insights for innovations during their dreams. The Russian chemist Dmitri Mendeleyev laid out the final form of the periodic table during a dream. German chemist Friedrich Kekulé discovered the arrangement of the benzene molecule during his sleep. Mary Shelley literally dreamed up *Frankenstein,* and Robert Lewis Stevenson received *Dr. Jekyll and Mr. Hyde* while asleep. Architect Solange Fabi o designed the Museum of Ocean and Surf during a dream. Gandhi's call for a non-violent movement to force the British from India came as a dream. Beethoven, Billy Joel and many other musicians received songs in their sleep.

So, if sleep is the time best suited for creative problem solving in God's beautifully designed brain, and if one-third of our lives is spent sleeping, would it not be dreadfully poor stewardship of God to *not* speak to us in our dreams? Would it also be dreadfully poor stewardship for God's appointed guardians—parents—*not* to train their children to be ready to hear the still, small voice of God calling them in the night? As Samuel said, "Speak, Lord, for your servant is listening" (1 Sam. 3:9).

Seeding Dreams and Incubating Solutions

Harvard psychologist Deirdre Barrett, who has studied the seeding of dreams for more than a decade, found that by reflecting on specific problems right before sleep, a person can increase chances of dreaming up solutions. In one experiment, she assigned homework to students, asking them to focus on a handful of problems right before bedtime. At the end of a week, nearly half of the students had dreamed about the problems, and about a quarter had dreamed up answers.

Barrett's advice for incubating dreams includes intentionally seeding a particular problem (a process she calls "dream incubation") and inviting the dream to bring a solution.[8] Taking Dr. Barrett's research to heart, the following are my thoughts on how to leverage the brilliance of the brain's design and incorporate it into the FAITH5 process. In this way, you can raise children into adults who will listen for the Holy Spirit's voice all night long—even in their dreams.

1. *Write down the problem.* Barrett suggests that people write down their problem as a brief phrase or sentence and place this note next to their bed. I suggest that you write down highs, lows and a one-sentence prayer in a journal that you place next to your bed.

2. *Review the problem.* A few minutes before going to bed, review the problem with your family or family of friends. Share both your highs and lows along with the Bible verse of the week. Then talk, pray and bless.

3. *Visualize the problem.* Barrett suggests that once a person is in bed, he or she should visualize the problem as a concrete image. I suggest picturing the problem as a clumsy dinosaur and the solution as a hungry little Pac-Man or piranha about to eat it to bits. Think of the problem like a storm cloud and pray for the Holy Spirit to blow it away during the night. Think of it as a frightened giant with no friends, and picture yourself as being brave enough to climb up his ear and offer to help solve his problem. Solving his could solve yours!

4. *Tell yourself you want to dream about the problem.* As you drift off to sleep, tell your family and God that you would like an answer. Whisper or sing the Bible verse again as you fall asleep.

5. *When you awake, try to recall the dream.* Barrett states that when a person awakens, he or she should lie quietly before getting out of bed in an effort to recall any trace of a dream, and then write it down. You can ask God, "So, what are You trying to say to me? What do You want me to do?"

Another idea is to picture yourself dreaming about the problem and then awakening and writing it down. You can tell God, "I'm going to sleep now, and I'd like to pick up the answer in the morning so that I can do Your will in Your way tomorrow. Speak, Lord, your servant is listening!"

You can also arrange objects connected to the problem on your night table or on the wall across from your bed. Add an inspirational poster, a photo of your family, a picture of Jesus, a statue of a guardian angel, or any symbols that comfort you and remind you of God's care. Don't think of these as icons or magical objects of worship, but just use them as aides to your memory, faith and dreams.

If you teach your children to do this and model it for them every night, you will enable them to develop the healthy habit of letting go and letting God take control. They will be physically, emotionally and spiritually better off the rest of their lives. Further, they'll grow up believing that God is on duty all night long and that they can pick up the answer in the morning.

Tech Rules So that Tech Doesn't Rule

I need to say something about tech use, cell phones and sleep. Two of the frightening and sad realities of our youth culture today are that most teens go to sleep with a precious and sinister sleep-stealing device within arm's reach, and most can't *not* answer a text from a friend. That means that whoever is the least healthy and most emotionally needy person in their circle of friends will set the rules for how late the whole group stays awake. One insomniac will affect and infect the whole lot. If the phone is in their room, your children will only be as healthy as their *least* healthy friend.

We previously discussed the necessity of sleep for the brain and the effects that lack of sleep have on a person's moods, brain function and overall physical, mental and emotional health. The National Sleep Foundation (NSF) calls sleep "food for the brain." In an article titled "Teens and Sleep," the NSF states that teens need 9.25 hours of sleep to function best, yet only 15 percent are getting 8.5 hours.[9] Lack of sleep limits the brain's ability to learn, leads to aggressive behavior, causes weight gain, contributes to illness, causes 100,000 traffic accidents a year, and—be sure to tell your child this one—makes people more prone to pimples![10]

As a parent who wants the best for your children, consider sitting down with them tonight and having the following strategic conversation. Tell them that you, as an adult with a fully developed prefrontal cortex (judgment center) in your brain, have weighed the evidence of what tech does to sleep and have come to an irrevocable decision concerning cell phone usage in your home.

Remind your children that just like the car, the cell phone does not belong to them. It is yours. You bought it, you are paying the monthly bill for it, so you own it. However, out of the kindness of your benevolent and generous heart, you might choose to let them use *your* phone as long as they follow three simple rules. If they break any of these rules, you will put the cell phone away for a week. These three rules are:

RULE 1: *Your* phone will be in *your* possession from 9 PM until 7 AM. (Aren't you generous to let them use *your* phone 14 hours each day?)

RULE 2: Your children will put *your* phone on the counter in the kitchen or into your hands by 9 PM each night. It will be waiting for them in the morning.

RULE 3: When you text or call them, they will answer. After all, why should you pay for a communication device if the person you lend it to doesn't communicate with you?

As long as we are on the topic of tech and sleep, there is one simple and inexpensive solution you can immediately implement to help the sleep-starved young people in your home: get the tech out of the bedroom. All of it! Now! No computer. No television. No Internet. No electronic games. No cell phones. No excuses. Let your children nag, whine and complain all they want. You will be giving them a life-long gift, and they will feel better about it in the morning. Every morning.

Parents of young children will find it easier to do this. Start early, stay firm, and it will simply become the norm. Parents of teenagers who are already addicted to the squirts of dopamine (pleasure drug) that accompany every "beep" of a text or "blip" of a game will have a tougher time, but they have to be tougher than the tough time.

Expect most children and teens to object. After all, that's in their job description. As a wise and loving parent, you have to stay firm, because you know what is at stake. That's in your job description.

The first time you enforce the no-tech-zone rules will be the most difficult. Count on it. It will get easier and easier every night from then on as your children realize that you are not going to budge on what you know to be in their best interests. Two other phrases you might want to get used to uttering out loud are:

1. "We will reconsider these rules when you have a fully developed prefrontal cortex [age 25 for girls and age 27 for boys]."
2. "We will reconsider these rules when you are paying all of your own bills."

Remind them of the Golden Rule: The one who has the gold makes the rules!

A FAITH5 Family Story

Does FAITH5 work? As for me and my house, I can testify from personal experience that it worked for us. First, my wife, Arlyce Joy, is still married to me. Now there's a reason to believe in miracles!

As for our children, I can say that they grew up into wonderful young adults whom my wife and I absolutely enjoy. We can't wait to have them home, and we treasure our time together. In high school, both kids invested their lives in church, in leadership in youth group, and in multiple Mexican mission trips, where they put roofs on hurricane-ravaged homes, schools and churches.

As of this writing, Kathryn Elizabeth is donating a second post-college year to a second homeless shelter—this one for teens in Denver, Colorado. Most of the youth she works with were abused, ran away from home, or were thrown out. Joseph Martin is a college student majoring in philosophy and political science. He donates his musical talents and fun-instigating personality to a summer Christian children's camp.

Although we have our differences—as healthy adults and good friends often do—both of our children have grown into adults with huge hearts for the poor, the outcasts, and the kind of people Jesus loved and ministered to most. Their friends and even casual acquaintances seek them out for wisdom, advice and counsel, knowing the depths of their honest love and care. This kind of loving and giving is not just what they do but who they are at the core.

To what can we attribute these wonderful, funderful, thunderful young adults who bring us such joy? To the grace of God? Yes, yes and yes. To good genes? Okay, I'll buy that. To quality care-giving surrogate aunts and uncles, teachers and pastors in our circle of friends at church? Yeah, that too. All of the above and then some.

I don't know the exact ratios of nature and nurture, of genes, epigenes and upbringing, but I do believe with all my heart that the nightly art of parenting and the enrichual faith practices we embedded every night had a lot to do with how our kids turned out. As in the little house on the prairie where I grew up with a teacher mom and a story-telling dad, we incubated faith, and faith incubated us. Night after night our prayer list grew. Night after night our care list grew. Night after night our aware and share list grew. Night after night our capacity to love grew, our faith grew, our children grew and we did too.

One prayer at a time. One care at a time. One night at a time.

Oh yeah, and one pillow fight at a time.

A Note on *Préjà Vu*

If you are raising a child today, you are sure to run into your own unique set of major-league challenges. Maybe these challenges haven't hit you yet, but if you are a parent—or soon to be one—they are on their way!

I call this kind of parental preparation and thinking *préjà vu.* It hasn't happened yet, but it's going to! You may wish to "pray it forward" and get started right away.

Maybe your parenting challenges won't be as tough as the families mentioned in each of the FAITH5 family stories in this book. Maybe they will be worse. Maybe you'll breeze through parenting blessed with easy children and normal wear and tear and prayer problems. Maybe you'll run into more than your share of heart-breaking challenges—problems that could shake you, break you and make you. Challenges that could test you, arrest you and maybe best you. Challenges that slap you in the face and slap you in the faith. Challenges that shake you to the core and possibly more. Challenges that either knock you on your back or knock you to your knees.

Like most families, mine had its share of troubles, challenges, scares, scars, broken hearts and visits to Christian counselors. There were nights when my kids didn't want to talk and the only high my wife could utter was, "Jesus loves me. Next!" There were nights when the FAITH5 ritual was the only glue that held our family together—especially when our children were teens.

In times like these, we needed to remember that we had a God who was bigger than our biggest problems. We had Jesus, for whom the grave was not even the end. We had the Holy Spirit, who was cheering for us with loving sighs deeper than words can express. I have stated this before, but it was so important for us to remember that we had a promise from God that if we were to train up our children in the way they should go, then when they are old they will not depart from it (see Prov. 22:6). We had to remember and hold fast to the hope that the Word of God is true and the will of God for us was that our family would come through the trials with beauty, depth, strength, resilience and joy. We had to know this, believe this and trust in this promise with all our hearts.

When my wife was nursing our babies and putting them to sleep, she filled every night with quiet love songs like "Children of the Heavenly Father," "Oh, How I Love Jesus," and "Jesus Loves Me, This I Know." I believe those early songs of faith etched themselves deeply into our children's little brains and that those first songs imprinted will be the last songs they hear when death draws near. Everything I know about neurology, psychology, sociology and theology tells me this is most certainly true. There is old proverb that holds true: "The songs that are sung in the cradle go to the grave."

One of my most frequent and fervent prayer blessings when our children were little was, "May you grow to be strong, loving and wise." God is answering that prayer at this very moment. We know it. We see it. We seeded it. And now Arlyce Joy and I couldn't be prouder. Our children have enriched our lives beyond measure. I know, believe and trust that long after we are gone, our children will continue to bless the world by caring for the kind of downtrodden people with whom Jesus spent most of His time. If I die tomorrow, I can live with that.

Plant the Seeds and Let God Do the Rest

With this book, I pray that I have prepared you to face these challenges proactively with intention and flare. I hope you are now ready to put some key safety nets in place using these nightly faith practices. I pray that you won't let a night pass by without getting into the face and the faith of those you love to engage in these beautiful, intimate, enriching and important bonding steps.

Once again, I want to reiterate that you will have the best results if you seek out a community of faith to join you on this journey. You need people who will commit and covenant together with you to face these coming challenges arm in arm, hand in hand, face to face, faith to faith and prayer in prayer. Create a Dream Team of allies—a critical mass to help you deal with what could be a critical mess. Start with other parents who have children your children's age. Add an elder or two for wisdom and experience, some empty-nesters for perspective and advice, a young adult or two as an aunt or uncle for your children, and a caring pastor for moral support.

If you have been blessed with the honor and the call of parenting today, you must know that there will be conflict. Count on it. There will be trials and tests. Expect them, but don't even think of facing them alone. There will be fiery trials that will purify the gold in your relationship if you simply hold on! Winston Churchill once said, "When going through hell, keep going."

As you face trials, remember that you have a God who is bigger than your biggest problem. You have Jesus, for whom the grave was not even the end. You have the Holy Spirit, who is cheering for you with loving sighs deeper than words can express. I have stated this before, but it is so important to remember: You have a promise from God that if you "train up a child in the way he should go, when he is old he will not depart from it." The Word of God is true, and the will of God is for your family to come through the challenges you face with beauty, depth, strength, resilience and joy. Trust in this promise. Rest in this promise. Rejoice in this promise. Hang on to this promise.

You plant the seeds. Let God provide the sun and the rain. You till the soil and pull the weeds. Let God do the work on the inside. Your job is to pray prayers. God's job is to answer them on God's time. The job of the Holy Spirit is already taken. Your job is to be faithful to your calling. God's job is to complete the work on God's schedule.

A few years ago, I took a screenwriting class from my friend Dr. Ted Baehr at www.movieguide.org. I learned one thing that stuck out: When it comes to writing a great screenplay, if there is no conflict, there is no story. The greater the conflict, the greater the struggle; and the greater the enemy, the greater the story and the more marvelous the ending!

If you want a great family story, don't pray for calm and wind-less seas. Pray for a great Captain. Prepare for a great conflict. Build yourself a sturdy ship. Gather a worthy and committed crew. Then launch into the tempest surrounded by the best, ready for the worst, embracing the storms with everything you've got to make yours a great and powerful story with an absolutely awesome ending!

As for You and Your Household

So, as for you and your household, will FAITH5 work? Here is what I know: Parents, you will see what you seed and reap what you sow. There will always be reasons not to start, but there will never be a better time to start than tonight. It won't be easier to begin tomorrow or the next night. Tonight's the night. Begin.

As I've said, the power of ritual is that it can hold you when you cannot hold yourself. Neurologically, it is not only emotion that leads to motion; motion—even when you don't feel like it—can lead to the emotion of care. The sharing of highs and lows, the caring conversations you have, and the holding of hands and hearts in prayer and blessing will change your family for the good. It will change your children's lives. Their perspective. Their respect. Their compassion. Their capacity for communication. Their capacity for care. Their understanding of the past. Their ability to hope, to cope, and to create the kind of future they hope to one day see.

You wouldn't forget to feed your children tonight, so don't starve them spiritually. You wouldn't leave your children unclothed tonight, so don't leave them emotionally and spiritually threadbare and cold. If you have time for three hours of tech and texting, you certainly have five minutes for doing FAITH5.

Don't let tonight go by without giving this gift, this bread, this power, this Jesus to your child and yourself. These are eternal gifts you will give to your children and to your children's children if you simply start right tonight. He who began the good work in you will be faithful to complete it. But you still have to show up.

Endnotes

Introduction: Sleeping in Heavenly Peace
1. Watch the Eustis video at www.faith5.org/intro/story.
2. John J. Ratey, *Spark: The Revolutionary New Science of Exercise and the Brain* (New York: Little, Brown and Company, 2008), p. 38.

Step 1: Share
1. Remember that any time is better than no time for sharing highs and lows. After school, around the dinner table and in the car might all work well for your family, but the optimal time to set the stage for maximum meaning-making in the human brain is in those few minutes right before you close your eyes and drift off to sleep.
2. Watch the Worthington video at www.faith5.org/share.
3. Enjoy a myriad of Melheimian Maxims at www.doctorrich.com.
4. A. C. Parks, Porta Della, R. S. Pierce , et al, "Pursuing Happiness in Everyday Life: The Characteristics and Behaviors of Online Happiness Seekers," May 28, 2012, online paper.
5. Martin Luther, *The Book of Concord: The Large Catechism.* http://bookofconcord.org/lc-3-tencommandments.php#para24.
6. American Psychological Association, "Stressed in America," January 2011. http://www.apa.org/monitor/2011/01/stressed-america.aspx.
7. American Psychological Association, "Our Health at Risk," March 2012. http://www.apa.org/monitor/2012/03/stress.aspx.
8. Answers.com, "How Many People Die in a Year Because of Stress?" http://wiki.answers.com/Q/How_many_people_die_in_a_year_because_of_stress.
9. Stressless.com, "Stress Related Facts." http://www.stressless.com/stressinfo.cfm.
10. Ibid.
11. Ibid.
12. Watch the cartoon and listen to the song at http://www.youtube.com/watch?v=b7qOFB4IXA8.
13. Andrew B. Newberg and Mark Robert Waldman, *Words Can Change Your Brain* (New York: Penguin Group, 2012), p. 12.
14. Nicholas Carr, *The Shallows: What the Internet Is Doing to Our Brains* (New York: W. W. Norton, 2011), p. 23.
15. Ibid., pp. 35, 45.
16. Louann Brizendine, MD, *The Female Brain* (New York: Broadway Books/Random House, 2006), p. 5.
17. Woman's Passion, "Women Speak Three Times More than Men," November 29, 2006. http://www.womanspassions.com/articles/570.html (accessed December 2012).
18. Andrew B. Newberg and Mark Robert Waldman, *Words Can Change Your Brain: 12 Conversation Strategies to Build Trust, Resolve Conflict, and Increase Intimacy* (New York: Hudson Street Press/Penguin Group, 2012), p. 4.
19. It has been 15 years since Amy's congregation took the brave step of cancelling their parentless age-segregated drop-off Sunday school and enlisting parents into the primary role of faith mentors for their own children. Faith Lutheran in West Fargo, North Dakota, promotes the church as reinforcement—not replacement—of the parents' duties. Over the years, FAITH5 has become the core of the nightly family faith engagement at Faith Lutheran. Visit them at www.growinfaith.org.

20. Richard Wiseman, *59 Seconds: Think a Little, Change a Lot* (New York: Alfred A. Knopf/ Random House, 2009), p. 297.

Step 2: Read

1. Watch the Gillund video at www.faith5.org/read.
2. History Learning Site, "The Seige of Leningrad." http://www.historylearningsite.co.uk/ siege_of_leningrad.htm.
3. *"GCB"* (TV series), Wikipedia.org. http://en.wikipedia.org/wiki/GCB_(TV_series)
4. "The M2 Generation: Are Your Kids Too Dependent on the Media?" Life.FamilyEducation.com. http://life.familyeducation.com/computers/television/65248.html#.ULIOlQ-RSS4.facebook.
5. "Media Education, *Pediatrics: Official Journal of the American Academy of Pediatrics.* http:// pediatrics.aappublications.org/content/104/2/341.full.htm.
6. Norman Herr, "The Sourcebook for Teaching Science," Television and Health. http:// www.csun.edu/science/health/docs/tvandhealth.html.
7. "Senate Committee on the Judiciary, Children, Violence, and the Media: a Report for Parents and Policy Makers," September 14, 1999. Previously available at http://judiciary.senate.gov/oldsite/mediavio.htm.
8. J. Federman, ed., *National Television Violence Study,* vol. 3 (Thousand Oaks, CA: Sage Publications, 1998).
9. Ibid.
10. F. Yokota and K. M. Thompson, "Violence in G-rated Animated Films," *The Journal of the American Medical Association,* May 24–31, 2000, vol. 283, no. 20, pp. 2716-2720.
11. American Academy of Pediatrics, Committee on Public Education, "Media Violence," *Pediatrics,* November 2001, vol. 108, no. 5, pp. 1222-1226.
12. B. J. Bushman and C. A. Anderson, "Comfortably Numb: Desensitizing Effects of Violent Media on Helping Others," *Psychological Science,* 2009, vol. 21, no. 3, pp. 273-277.
13. L. R. Huesmann, J. Moise-Titus, C. L. Podolski and L. D. Eron, "Longitudinal Relations Between Children's Exposure to TV Violence and Their Aggressive and Violent Behavior in Young Adulthood, 1977–1992," *Developmental Psychology,* March 2003, vol. 39, no. 2, pp. 201-221.
14. University of Michigan Home Study. http://www.med.umich.edu/yourchild/topics/ tv.htm.
15. Bushman and Anderson, "Comfortably Numb: Desensitizing Effects of Violent Media on Helping Others."
16. J. G. Johnson, P. Cohen, E. M. Smailes, et al, "Television Viewing and Aggressive Behavior During Adolescence and Adulthood," *Science,* March 29, 2002, vol. 295, no. 5564, pp. 2468-2471.
17. J. A. Manganello and C. A. Taylor, "Television Exposure as a Risk Factor for Aggressive Behavior Among Three-year-old Children," *Archives of Pediatrics and Adolescent Medicine,* November 2009, vol. 163, no. 11, pp. 1037-1045.
18. University of Michigan Home Study. http://www.med.umich.edu/yourchild/topics/ tv.htm.
19. Facing the Future, "Consumption Fast Facts and Quick Actions," http://www.facingthefuture.org/ServiceLearning/FastFactsQuickActions/Consumption/tabid/176/Default.aspx; *CBS Sunday Morning,* "Cutting Through Advertising Clutter," http:// www.cbsnews.com/8301-3445_162-2015684.html.
20. Sherry Turkel, *Alone Together* (New York: Perseus Books, 2011), p. 203.
21. Ibid., p. 152.

22. Ibid., p. 156.
23. Ibid., p. 225.
24. Kevin Kelly, "Technophilia," *The Technium*, June 8, 2009. http://www.kk.org/thetech nium/archives/2009/06/technophilia.php.
25. Chocolatefrog, "Beautiful," Teen Ink Webzine, Derry, Ireland. http://www.teen ink.com/hot_topics/what_matters/article/463898/Beautiful.
26. Just for Women, "Did You Know?" http://www.confidencecoalition.org/statistics-women.
27. Girl Scouts, "Physical and Mental Health." http://www.girlscouts.org/research/facts_findings/physical_and_mental_health.asp.
28. Do Something.org, "11 Facts about Teens and Self Esteem." http://www.dosome thing.org/tipsandtools/11-facts-about-teens-and-self-esteem.
29. Leonard Sax, *Boys Adrift: The Five Factors Driving the Growing Epidemic of Unmotivated Boys and Underachieving Young Men* (New York: Basic Books, 2009).
30. Center for Disease Control and Prevention, "Childhood Overweight and Obesity." http://www.cdc.gov/obesity/childhood.
31. Léon Dumond, quoted in Nicholas Carr, *The Shallows: What the Internet Is Doing to Our Brains* (New York: W. W. Norton & Company, 2011), p. 21.
32. Ibid., p. 27.
33. Ibid., p. 34.
34. Roma Downey and Mark Burnett, "Why Public Schools Should Teach the Bible," *The Wall Street Journal*, U. S. edition, March 1, 2013, p. A11.
35. StarTribune, "Obituary for Ross Alan Florand," July 12, 2009. http://www.legacy.com/obituaries/startribune/obituary.aspx?page=lifestoryandpid=129644959.
36. The downloadable lessons are available at www.faith5.org/extras. One hundred percent of the profits from sales of these 22 themes, skits and discussion guides will go to-ward bringing God's Word in song and dance to orphan children in India.

Step 3: Talk

1. The *FAITH5 Home Huddle Journals* can be viewed at www.faith5.org/resources.
2. Watch the Diamond video at www.faith5.org/talk.
3. Nicholas Carr, *The Shallows: What the Internet Is Doing to Our Brains* (New York: W. W. Norton, 2011), p. 51.
4. Ibid., p. 55.
5. Sjeila E. Crowell, "The Neurobiology of Declarative Memory," quoted in John H. Schu-mann, Sheila E. Crowell, Nancy E. Jones, et al., *The Neurobiology of Learning: Perspectives from Second Language Acquisition* (Mahway, NJ: Erlbaum, 2004), p. 76.
6. Nicholas Carr, *The Shallows: What the Internet Is Doing to Our Brains*, p. 192.
7. Gerald Edelman, *Bright Air, Brilliant Fire* (New York: Basic Books, 1992), p. 17.
8. "Secondary Consciousness," Wikipedia.org. http://en.wikipedia.org/wiki/Secondary_consciousness.
9. Stuart Kauffman, quoted in "The Genius of the Tinkerer," *Wall Street Journal*, Septem-ber 25, 2010. http://online.wsj.com/article/SB10001424052748703989304575503730101860838.html.
10. Steven Johnson, *Where Good Ideas Come From: The Natural History of Innovation* (New York: Penguin Group, 2010), p. 2.
11. The Independent, "Life 'Meaningless' for One in 10 Young Adults," January 5, 2009. http://www.independent.co.uk/life-style/health-and-families/health-news/life-mean ingless-for-one-in-10-young-adults-1226329.html.

12. Phil Callaway, *Who Put My Life on Fast-Forward? How to Slow Down and Start Living Again* (Eugene, OR: Harvest House Publishers, 2002), p. 10.
13. Haptic technology adds touch to the virtual experience (see http://en.wikipedia.org/wiki/Haptic_technology). Holodeck technology allows one to experience a virtual world in 3D (see http://www.huffingtonpost.co.uk/2012/07/23/project-holodeck-could-tu_n_1695329.html).
14. Andrew B. Newberg, MD, and Mark Robert Waldman, *Words Can Change Your Brain: 12 Conversation Strategies to Build Trust, Resolve Conflict, and Increase Intimacy* (New York: Penguin, 2012), p. 4.
15. Sherry Turkel, *Alone Together* (New York: Perseus Books, 2011), p. 156.
16. David G. Meyers, *Exploring Psychology* (New York: Worth Books, 2005), p. 392.
17. A. Todorov, "Evaluating Faces on Trustworthiness: an Extension of Systems for Recognition of Emotions Signaling Approach/Avoidance Behaviors," *Annals of the New York Academy of Sciences,* March 2008, vol. 1124, pp. 208-224.
18. A. D. Engell, A. Todorov and J. V. Haxby, "Common Neural Mechanisms for the Evaluation of Facial Trustworthiness and Emotional Expressions as Revealed by Behavioral Adaptation," *Perception,* 2010 vol. 39, no. 7, pp. 931-441.
19. Andrew B. Newberg and Mark Robert Waldman, "Words Can Change Your Brain," *Psychology Today.* http://www.psychologytoday.com/blog/words-can-change-your-brain/201207/the-8-key-elements-highly-effective-speech.
20. "Albert Mehrabian," Wikipedia.org. http://en.wikipedia.org/wiki/Albert_Mehrabian.

Step 4: Pray

1. Watch the Ogden video at www.faith5.org/pray/story.
2. Sherry Turkle, *Alone Together* (New York: Perseus Books, 2011), p. 56.
3. Some of my favorite sites for simple children's prayers include the following: (1) http://christianity.about.com/od/prayersforspecificneeds/qt/morningprayers.htm; (2) http://www.apples4theteacher.com/childrens-prayers/morning; (3) http://www.lords-prayer-words.com/prayers_before/good_morning_prayers.html.

Step 5: Bless

1. Watch the tribute *Pastor Ray's Last Days* at www.faith5.org/bless/story.
2. Carl Rogers, "The Interpersonal Relationship: The Core of Guidance," quoted in Raymond M. Maslowski and Lewis B. Morgan, eds., "Interpersonal Growth and Self Actualization in Groups," MSS Information Corporation, pp. 176-189.
3. Abraham H. Maslow, "Peak Experiences as Acute Identity Experiences," *American Journal of Psychoanalysis,* vol. 21, pp. 254-260.
4. Happy Feet Reflexology, "Enjoy a Happy, Healthy, Stress-Free State of Being." http://www.rockvillehappyfeet.com/reflexology.html.
5. Read the entire email exchange between Karen and me at faith5.org/extras.
6. For you theologians out there, the Hebrew word for blessing, *barak*, means to kneel or bow with bended knee. One would bow humbly in the presence of the holy to receive divine gifts and favor. The English word "blesses" stems from the Anglo-Saxon *blestain* or *bledsian*, from which we also get the word "blood." In ancient ceremonies, sacrificial blood was shed to bond a covenant, forgive sins and make a person or thing holy and acceptable to God.
7. Paul Simon, "I Am a Rock," on the album *Sound of Silence* (CBS Records, 1965). Watch Simon and Garfunkel sing this song at http://www.youtube.com/watch?v=My9I8q-iJCI.
8. "List of Serial Killers by Number of Victims, Wikipedia.org. http://en.wikipedia.org/wiki/List_of_serial_killers_by_number_of_victims.

9. Mark Follman, Gavin Aronsen and Deanna Pan, "A Guide to Mass Shootings in America," Mother Jones, February 27, 2013. http://www.motherjones.com/politics/2012/07/mass-shootings-map.

10. Frank Hammond, *The Father's Blessing* (Kirkwood, MO: Impact Christian Books, 2011), p. 3.

11. Paul Dobransky, MD, "The Urban Scientist: If You Don't Have a Father Today," *Psychology Today*, June 21, 2009. http://www.psychologytoday.com/blog/the-urban-scientist/200906/if-you-dont-have-father-today-0.

12. Edward Kruk, Ph.D., "Coparenting After Divorce," *Psychology Today*. http://www.psychologytoday.com/blog/co-parenting-after-divorce/201205/father-absence-father-deficit-father-hunger.

13. "Statistics," The Fatherless Generation. http://thefatherlessgeneration.wordpress.com/statistics.

14. Esther Meeks, *Loving to Know: Introducing Covenant Epistemology* (Eugene, OR: Cascade Books, 2011).

Epilogue: Why Nighttime Is the Right Time

1. Vibrant Faith Ministries, "Vibrant Faith Frame." http://www.vibrantfaith.org/documents/VFM_6543_Flyer10.23.09.pdf; "102," Faith Formation 2020, http://www.faithformation2020.net/index.htm.

2. Lifelong Faith Associates. http://www.lifelongfaith.com.

3. David B. Agus, MD., *The End of Illness* (New York: Free Press, 2011), p. 240.

4. S. Miano, P. Parisi and M. P. Villa, "The Sleep Phenotypes of Attention Deficit Hyperactivity Disorder: The Role of Arousal During Sleep and Implications for Treatment," *Medical Hypotheses,* August 2012, vol. 79, no. 2, pp. 147-153.

5. Quoted by Christa Hines in "Bonding at Bedtime," *Nashville Parent*, August 24, 2012. http://www.nashvilleparent.com/2012/08/bonding-at-bedtime.

6. John Medina, *Brain Rules: 12 Principles for Surviving and Thriving at Work, Home and School* (Seattle, WA: Pear Press, 2008), p. 152.

7. Sara Mednik, quoted in U. C. San Diego News Center, "Let Me Sleep on It: Creative Problem Solving Enhanced by REM Sleep," June 9, 2009. http://ucsdnews.ucsd.edu/newsrel/health/06-09Mednick.asp (accessed January 2013).

8. Deirdre Barrett, "Answers in Your Dreams," *Scientific American Mind*, November/December, 2011, p. 32.

9. National Sleep Foundation, "Teens and Sleep." http://www.sleepfoundation.org/article/sleep-topics/teens-and-sleep (accessed March 2013).

10. Ibid.

One-Year Bible Schedule in Songs, Sign and Games

Here's a fun way to engage Scripture with your family Bible every night. After sharing highs and lows, grab your Bibles and read and highlight each theme verse. Then hop online to www.faithink.com and enter the suggested FINKlink Code to learn the Scripture in song, American Sign Language and games. If you really want to experience God's Word in all its richness, instead of choosing a different verse each night, stick to the same Scripture all week long. By the end of the week, you will know it by heart in both song and sign language for the rest of your life! (Note: There is an entire Christian education curricula for home and church built on these resources. Check them out at www.faith5.org/curricula. For the FINKlink codes, go to www. faithink.com and enter in the FINKlink box.)

Introduction to FAITH5

Week	Theme Song	Verse	FINKlink Code
1	Sleep in Peace (Introduction)	Ps. 4:8	SI01
2	Where Can I Go? (Share)	Ps. 139:7	SI15
3	Word in My Heart (Read)	Pss. 19:8,11,105; 122:1	SI14
4	Keep These Words (Talk)	Deut. 6:4-10	BM15
5	As I Pray My Vows (Pray)	Ps. 61:1-5,8	SI10
6	The Lord Bless You (Bless)	Num. 6:24-26	BM13

Unit 1: The Books of Moses

Week	Theme Song	Verse	FINKlink Code
7	Let There Be Light	Gen. 1:1-3	BM01
8	Where Are You?	Gen. 3:8-9	BM03
9	Bow in the Clouds	Gen. 9:7,13-15; 8:22	BM03
10	Look to Heaven	Gen. 15:5	BM04
11	God Will Provide	Gen. 22:1-3a,6-8	BM05
12	Jake's Dream	Gen. 28:11-14	BM06
13	Son of His Old Age	Gen. 37:3-4, 23-24,28,34-35; 50:20a	BM07
14	Burning Bush	Exod. 3:1-2, 6-7,11,13	BM08
15	Take a Lamb	Exod. 12:3,5a, 6b-7,12-13	BM09
16	Into the Sea	Exod. 15:1-2, 9-12	BM10
17	I Am	Exod. 20:2-3	BM11
18	You Shall Be Holy	Lev. 19:2b; 10:3	BM12
19	Will He Not?	Num. 23:19	BM14

Check out the "Books of Moses" home journal at
http://www.faithink.com/Inkubators/biblesong_book_moses_journal.asp

Unit 2: Into the Promised Land

Week	Theme Song	Verse	FINKlink Code
20	Be Strong!	Josh. 1:5b,9	PL01
21	As for Me	Josh. 24:15	PL02

Week	Theme Song	Verse	FINKlink Code
22	Hear, O Kings	Judg. 5:3	PL03
23	Where You Go	Ruth 1:16	PL04
24	God Looks on the Heart	1 Sam. 16:7	PL05
25	Goliath's Requiem	1 Sam. 17:45-46a,47b	PL06
26	David Danced	2 Sam. 6:14; 22:1-20	PL07
27	Solomon's Prayer	1 Kings 8:27,30	PL08
28	I Know Your Rising	2 Kings 19:27a	PL09
29	Declare His Glory	1 Chron. 16:24, 31-34	PL10
30	If My People	2 Chron. 7:14	PL11
31	For He Is Good	Ezra 3:10-11b	PL12
32	Strengthen My Hands	Nehemiah 6:9c	PL13
33	The Deep Things	Job 11:7-12	PL15
34	He Has Done It	Ps. 22:27,29-31	SI0
35	O Taste and See	Ps. 34:4-8	SI06
36	A Thousand Years	Ps. 90:4-5, 9-10,12	SI11

Check out the "Into the Promised Land" home journal at
http://www.faithink.com/Inkubators/biblesong_book_promised_journal.asp

Unit 3: The Good News

Week	Theme Song	Verse	FINKlink Code
37	In the Beginning	John 1:1-5, 9-12,14	GN01
38	Magnify the Lord	Luke 1:47-49	GN02

Week	Theme Song	Verse	FINKlink Code
39	Emmanuel	Matt. 1:20b-23	GN03
40	Prepare the Way	Matt. 3:1-3	GN04
41	Salt of the Earth	Matt. 5:3-10, 13a,14,16	GN05
42	Living Water	John 4:13-15; 7:38b	GN06
43	The Lord's Prayer	Matt. 6:9-13	GN07
44	Love the Lord	Mark 12:28-31a	GN08
45	Are You the One?	Matt. 11:3-5	GN09
46	I Am the Way	John 14:6	GN10
47	Love One Another	John 15:12-13	GN11
48	For God So Loved	John 3:16	GN12
49	Easter Morning	Mark 16:2-7	GN13
50	Stay with Us	Luke 24:29-32	GN14
51	Go Therefore	Matt. 28:19-20	GN15
52	You Will Receive Power	Acts 1:8	GN15

Check out the "Into the Promised Land" home journal at
http://www.faithink.com/Inkubators/biblesong_book_goodnews_journal.asp

Two years of additional Bible verses and songs (from Genesis 1 to Revelation 22) await you at www.faith5.org/bibleschedule.

FAITH5 Resources for Church and Home

There are seven FAITH5 resources for church and home waiting to enrich your parenting experience and help you strengthen your family. These include:

1. FAITH5 Facebook Site

Share your stories, struggles and strivings specifically related to parenting on this site. If you need a little encouragement from time to time, sign up and let's see if we can find you an international Dream Team of supporters to help you hold your family together. The only three criteria for postings are:

1. Be Positive
2. Be Brief
3. Be Honest

Join the conversation at www.facebook.com and type FAITH5 in the Search bar.

2. FAITH5 Blog

There's a FAITH5 blog with articles, links, video interviews, book reviews and more waiting to enrich and equip you in your parenting challenges. See what I am thinking and learning each week at www.faith5.org/blog.

3. FAITH5 Six-Week Course

Implement FAITH5 across the entire congregation in six sessions. The series includes:

- One preaching and teaching DVD
- Six PowerPoint presentations
- Six Bible songs with American Sign Language
- Six participant handouts
- Six family art projects
- Six bulletin inserts
- One set of promotional materials (posters, postcards, bulletin inserts) in pdf format

A free sample download of chapter 1 is available at www.faith5.org/course.

4. FAITH5 for Children—Bible Song Curriculum

Seventy-five Bible stories, games and songs await your home school or church school with the Bible song curriculum featuring FAITH5. Built on a PowerPoint base for projection, resources include music, art, games and cartoon handouts for small children, elementary school children, youth and adults. And don't forget the beautiful full-color cartoon home huddle journals. Themes include:

- The books of Moses (15 stories from the books of Genesis to Deuteronomy)
- Into the Promised Land (15 stories from Joshua to Job)
- The songs of Israel (15 psalms of David meet the parables of Jesus)
- The good news (15 stories from Matthew to John)
- The Word spreads (15 stories from the book of Acts and Scriptures chosen from the letters of Paul to take you from Acts to Philemon)

For free Bible song sample downloads, visit http://www.fai-think.com/Inkubators/biblesong_samples.asp.

5. FAITH5 for Youth—Head to the Heart

Here you will find 90 topical themes for Christian living with PowerPoint curriculum for teachers, handouts for youth, 90 Bible songs (verbatim), 90 online games, and 270 short online devotions. The series includes 90-page spiral bound FAITH5 Home Huddle Journals for teens and parents to do together each night. Themes include:

- The Old Testament (10 themes giving an overview of the mighty acts of God)
- The life of Jesus (10 themes from the birth of Jesus to the Great Commission)
- The New Testament (10 themes from Pentecost to the Revelation of John)
- The Ten Commandments (10 themes applying God's will to your world today)
- The Lord's Prayer (10 themes on the most powerful prayer of all time)
- The Apostles' Creed (10 themes on the Creator, Savior, Spirit and church)
- Hot topics (10 themes from sex to drugs to science to suicide and more)
- Plus John Calvin, Martin Luther, John Wesley and more

Free head to the heart sample downloads are available at http://www.faithink.com/Inkubators/h2h_samples.asp.

6. FAITH5 for Families—Faith Steppingstones

Enjoy these three-week mini-courses implementing FAITH5 at eight key stages of parenting. Resources come on PowerPoint with a curriculum for teachers, handouts, and eight blessing worship services for families to recommit to Christian parenting at every phase of family life. Here you will find courses geared toward all ages:

- Infants (teaching nightly blessing)
- Toddlers (teaching nightly prayer and blessing)
- Kindergartners (teaching nightly highs and lows, prayer and blessing)
- Early readers (teaching a nightly Bible verse each night, highs and lows, prayer and blessing)

- Preteens (teaching "I'm sorry" [nightly confession/absolution] plus the other parts of the FAITH5)
- Surviving adolescence (deepening all of the FAITH5 practices)
- Mid-adolescence (deepening the FAITH5 even further)
- Graduation (looking back, looking to the moment, looking ahead at living the Christian life, and spreading FAITH5 wherever you go)

Free video of each course available at http://www.faithink.com/Inkubators/steppingstones.asp.

7. FAITH5 for Cross-Generational Education and Worship

Adopt a cross-generational FAITH5 family for a season and learn Bible stories while sharing your nightly enrichuals with elders, children and others in the same community. Themes are built on the texts from the Revised Common Lectionary, cycles A, B and C. Resources include:

- FAITH5 for Advent
- FAITH5 for Lent
- FAITH5 for Stewardship

Learn more at http://www.faithink.com/Inkubators/gift.asp.

Acknowledgments

First, I'd like to thank my old seminary professor and role model, Dr. Roland Martinson, for his brilliant advice. Twenty years ago when I asked Rollie if I should pursue a doctorate, he told me, "Naw. Go get your education first."

I'd like to thank Dr. B. J. Jun, my dissertation advisor, for his grace, counsel and friendship; Pastor Dan Poffenberger, the good folks at George Fox Evangelical Seminary and the rest of my doctoral cohort, for their camaraderie and support; Bill Greig III at Regal, for testing these concepts with his own children and believing in the message enough to publish the book; Stan Jantz at Regal and David Shepherd, my literary agent, for their hard work and brilliant strategic advice; Mark Weising, my editor at Regal, for his advice, work and technical genius; and Ted and Robbie Baehr and the good folks at www.movieguide.org, for all their publicity assistance.

Thank you to the late Mike Yaconelli, for talking me into staying in youth ministry once when I was burning out; Drs. Dallas Willard, Tony Campolo and Bill Easum, for their willingness to let me pick their brains and capture their wisdom on video from time to time over the years; Todd Ernster, from *The Killer Hayseeds*, and all the FINK Music Guild members, for adding their talents to our 250 Bible verse songs; Christy Smith, from *Discovering Deaf Worlds,* for signing many of the songs in ASL; Tom Oswald at Rising Star Education and Janakan Arulkumarasan at www.onoko.com, for their encouragement and texpertise; Debbie Streicher, for years of friendship, family ministry insights and for dreaming up the FAITH5 name; and Monty Lysne, Tom Collins and the rest of the Faith Inkubators staff, for their endless patience, hard work and often under-appreciated efforts.

Immeasurable thanks go to my parents, Kathryn Marie and Raymond Edward Melheim, for teaching me how to live and then teaching me how to die. Thank you to my wife, Arlyce Joy, and children, Kathryn Elizabeth and Joseph Martin, for loving me in ways I needed to be loved, enriching my life in too many ways to number, and giving me a treasure bank of stories for the core of my work. And thank you to Jesus, for sending me back for one more assignment on the day my heart stopped. (Maybe I'll get it right this time.)

Finally, this book grew out of a doctoral dissertation in the field of semiotics and future studies, for which Dr. Leonard Sweet is to blame. I was too busy to even think of investing time in an advanced degree until Len showed up as a surprise guest at an Aspen think-tank I was hosting. "Your work isn't bad," he said, "but you should get some people smarter than you to take a look at it." A lot of smarter people and a doctorate later, I really must say Len was right. Thanks, Len.

About the Author

Dr. Rich Melheim grew up on the plains of North Dakota but never owned a pickup with a gun rack.

An author, composer, comedian, cartoonist, playwright, record producer, educational systems designer, curriculum developer and amateur student of the human brain, Rich has pastored churches, founded an international ministry (www.faithink.com), created an international model for brain-based preschools on arts-based platforms, and appeared on CNN, *The Osgood Files* and 50 network news channels from WNBC-New York to KTLA, counseling on parenting issues.

Rich holds a BA in Journalism from the University of North Dakota, a Masters of Divinity from Luther Seminary, and a Doctor of Ministry in Semiotics and the Future from George Fox Evangelical Seminary.

Rich has been married to his Bible camp sweetheart, Arlyce Joy, ever since he had a Norwegian Afro and a guitar strapped to his back. He enjoys the company of two wonderful and funderful adult children, Kathryn Elizabeth and Joseph Martin, and often tries to con them into traveling with him.

Rich blogs at www.faith5.org/blogs and writes for www.rich-learning.com. He can be reached on Facebook or emailed at info@faithink.com.

Find his vita and schedule at About.me/melheimrich.

I openly cried real tears and felt a spiritual uplifting deep within my soul when I read the influence Rich's mother had on their spirituality and general development. I want to purchase this book as special gifts to all my children and grandchildren.

Beverly A. Blackman-Mounce, Clifton, Texas

Funny . . . insightful . . . deep and heartfelt as well as humorous. This book offers a way families can reconnect with each other while returning God to the center of family life.

Christopher Byars, Zephyrhills, Florida

More families could use FAITH5 in this day of self-centeredness, greed and angst.

Chris Calhoun, Indiana, Pennsylvania

I like the humor. I could recommend this to a parent who doesn't feel confident reading a "theology" book and sense that they'd make sense of it. I want to read it with my team at church.

Michelle Collins, Melbourne, Florida

I started reading and couldn't stop. I was captivated. The chapter on blessing brought tears to my eyes and a lump to my throat as I read. I don't have grandchildren yet, but when I do, they will know they won't leave Gramma's house without a blessing. Actually, the next time my kids come home . . .

Darla Eeten, Boyden, Iowa

This will make a great book study for different groups at your church. I thought the section on the differences between boys and girls and getting them to share was helpful, and I appreciated the acknowledgment of absent parents.

Krista L. Henning-Ferkin, Libertyville, Illinois

After reading this book I talked with my husband about changing our nighttime routine to include FAITH5.

Paula Johnson, Pawleys Island, South Carolina

Dr. Rich Melheim

"Step 5: Bless" really spoke to me. I have an adopted daughter who is prone to rages. We had been doing a nightly blessing: "You are God's child. I love you. I'll see you in the morning." Reading this chapter has caused me to start doing it again. I also used the blessing in my sermon at my mother's memorial service. It gave me an anchor and a way of saying I will hold fast and trust God's promises.

Dave Hall, Sidney, Nebraska

The stuff about holographs and the future scares the bejeebers out of me. This book has given me so much to think about, and I'm excited about using it as a resource for families in my congregation, at home with my husband, and to give to nieces and nephews as they begin having families of their own.

Kris Franke Hill, San Antonio, Texas

As a retired teacher, I liked the science behind each of the FAITH5 areas, which gives validity to the five practices. It's interesting to understand how God has put us together and how we can benefit by using what He has given us correctly.

Beck Marchiando, Aurora, Illinois

This book creates the rationale for both highs and lows on different levels—psychological, theological and sociological. It explains the reasons why FAITH5 is such a cool experience for families and for use in youth groups at church.

Sister Jennie Myers, Wytheville, Virginia

This is a great manual for changing the world one family at a time. My child now follows the creases in her daddy's forehead when she blesses him goodnight!

Patti Morlcok, Reynoldsburg, Ohio

Gripping, frightening and compelling.

James Pancoast, Llano, Texas

Exceptional research! The section "The Mass, the Mess, the Message and the Massage" will hit parents right between the eyes. This book is an incredible gift to the advancement of God's kingdom.

Rod Pasch, Slidel, Lousiana

HOLDING YOUR
FAMILY
TOGETHER COURSE

A Healthier Family in Six Weeks

FEATURING THE
FAITH5

by Dr. Rich Melheim

If you liked the book, you'll

LOVE

the course...

When you find something particularly meaningful and helpful, you like to share it with your friends. Bring this gift to your small group, parenting group or your entire church with this fun six-week course designed to immerse the people you love in these healthy faith practices.
The course includes:

A Healthier Family in Six Weeks
- 1 DVD for Worship and Educational Settings
- 1 Leader's Guide
- 6 PowerPoint Presentations
- 6 Bible Songs with American Sign Language
- 6 Bulletin Inserts
- Promotional Materials (Posters, Post Cards)

Order the course at
www.faith5.org/course

Curricula for Church and Home

Care to go deeper into the Bible with music, arts, skits and games while connecting church to home?

Home Journals

Read the Bible stories, sing the Bible Songs, play the Bible games, then record your highs, lows and prayers every night with these beautifully crafted full-color bedside books.

Children and Family Journals
- The Books of Moses
- Into the Promised Land
- Psalms and Parables
- The Good News
- Word Spreads

Youth and Family Journals
- Lord's Prayer
- Ten Commandments
- Hot Topics
- Old Testament
- New Testament
- Life of Jesus
- Apostles' Creed
- And More

DOWNLOAD FREE SAMPLES

& ORDER JOURNALS at

www.faith5.org/resources

RESOURCES

THE LOST SHEEP

Story 4

SHEEP ARE NOT THE SMARTEST OF CREATURES. THEY WANDER OFF, NIBBLING THEMSELVES TO LOSTNESS AND OFTEN CAN'T SEEM TO FIND THEIR WAY BACK HOME.

WHEN THE LEAD SHEEP WALKS OVER A CLIFF, THE WHOLE HERD WILL SOMETIMES FOLLOW.

BAA!*

WHEN SHEEP FALL ON THEIR BACKS, THEY DON'T EVEN KNOW HOW TO TURN OVER AGAIN!

BAAAAA!**

BAAA!***

OF ALL THE SONGS OF ISRAEL, THE BEST-KNOWN AND BEST-LOVED HAPPENS TO BE ABOUT SHEEP AND A GOOD SHEPHERD!

THE LORD IS MY SHEPHERD, I SHALL NOT WANT.

HE MAKES ME LIE DOWN IN GREEN PASTURES; HE LEADS ME BESIDE STILL WATERS; HE RESTORES MY SOUL.

HE LEADS ME IN RIGHT PATHS FOR HIS NAME'S SAKE.

EVEN THOUGH I WALK THROUGH THE DARKEST VALLEY, I FEAR NO EVIL; FOR YOU ARE WITH ME; YOUR ROD AND YOUR STAFF - THEY COMFORT ME.

BLEET!****

BIBLE SONG

* SHEEP FOR: "LOOK! OUR ILLUSTRIOUS LEADER HAS WALKED OVER A CLIFF. LET US FOLLOW!" ** "YOU ARE TRULY WISE, O SHAGGY ONE!"

Enjoy Dr. Rich's cartoons for every Bible story with Bible Song handouts, then go online and learn the Scripture in Music and American Sign Language! Download free samples at www.faiths.org/resources.

Made in the USA
Monee, IL
05 October 2021